Lockheed SR-71
Blackbird

Lockheed SR-71
Blackbird

Paul F Crickmore

Published in 1986 by Osprey Publishing Limited
27A Floral Street, London WC2E 9L P
Member company of the George Philip Group
© Paul F Crickmore

Sole distributors for the USA

Motorbooks International
Publishers & Wholesalers Inc
Osceola, Wisconsin 54020, USA

British Library Cataloguing in Publication Data

Crickmore, Paul F.
    Lockheed SR-71 Blackbird.—(Osprey air combat)
    1. SR-71 (Jet reconnaissance plane)
    I. Title
    623.74'67   UG1242.R4

    ISBN 0-85045-735-1
    ISBN 0-85045-653-3 Pbk

Editor Dennis Baldry

Designed by Norman Brownsword

Filmset in Great Britain by Tameside Filmsetting
Limited, Ashton-under-Lyne, Lancashire and printed
by BAS Printers Limited, Over Wallop, Hampshire

FRONT COVER AND TITLE PAGES
*Lockheed SR-71A of Detachment 4, 9th Strategic
Reconnaissance Wing, 1st Strategic Reconnaissance
Squadron of the US Air Force based at RAF Mildenhall,
Suffolk, England (Paul F Crickmore)*

Contents

Foreword

When I flew escort for the Blackbird in the F-104, the end of my flight profile was an acceleration to Mach 2.0 and a climb to 50,000 ft (15,240 m) while heading back to Nevada. If I timed it right I could look up and see Bill Park in an overtake coming back from the Canadian border approaching his speed point. Knowing he had me by about 5 miles (8 km) in altitude and 1,000 mph (1610 km/h) in speed, I would shudder at the step we were taking. There I was at top speed as escort in a Starfighter, the airplane which held the official world speed and altitude records, being totally outclassed. On the next mission we would trade places and I would be back up there again. It was hard to believe we were actually doing this.

Clawing at the cloak of secrecy that shrouded this programme was futile until some 20 years had passed. The story now told so ably by the author, Paul Crickmore, reveals the magnitude of the technical achievement in the development of the Blackbird. Here is an airplane that lives in the upper right hand corner of its speed and altitude envelope, in a thermal thicket. It is there because that is where range parameters approach similar fuel economies in jets at subsonic cruising speed. It also offers a private sky in which to perform a military mission unmolested.

One thing apparent in this book is why a Mach 3 supersonic transport fleet will not replace the present generation of subsonic jet airliners—only the economics of the military mission make sense. With highly skilled pilots and maintenance the SR-71 continues to operate successfully today.

Like most test pilots, I dreamed of the day I would be in the right place at the right time. It did happen and I had the honour to make the first flight and subsequent test flights in a startling new airplane, the A-12 proof-of-concept vehicle which became the SR-71 Blackbird. Now, 25 years later in my twilight years, I am experiencing an additional thrill to write the foreword for this interesting book. The effort in doing the research for this story probably fits right in with the efforts of all the dedicated individuals which made the SR-71 programme another successful milestone in the aviation achievements of our country.

Louis W Schalk
McLean, Virginia
April 1986

A Soviet airbase photographed by a Lockheed U-2 spyplane flying at 72,000 ft (21,950 m), probably around 1958. Most of the aircraft in the lineup are Tupolev Tu-16s, plus a number of Myasishchyev M-4 long-range bombers
(CIA)

Introduction

At 06:26 on 1 May 1960, 'Dragon Lady', article number 360, climbed away from a base near Peshawar in Pakistan bound for Bodo in Norway. It did not arrive. Some 1,300 miles (2407 km) inside the Soviet Union, 'Operation Overflight' fell foul of developing Soviet missile technology and ended near Sverdlovsk. One Francis Gary Powers and his Lockheed U-2B became headline news around the world. The political ramifications of this incident were to have a lasting effect upon US peacetime aerial reconnaissance programme (Parpro) of the Soviet Union. Overflights of the Soviet Union by aircraft of the United States and the United Kingdom, carried out in a highly classified and rigidly controlled manner for 15 years, would now cease.

The purpose of these secret flights can be traced

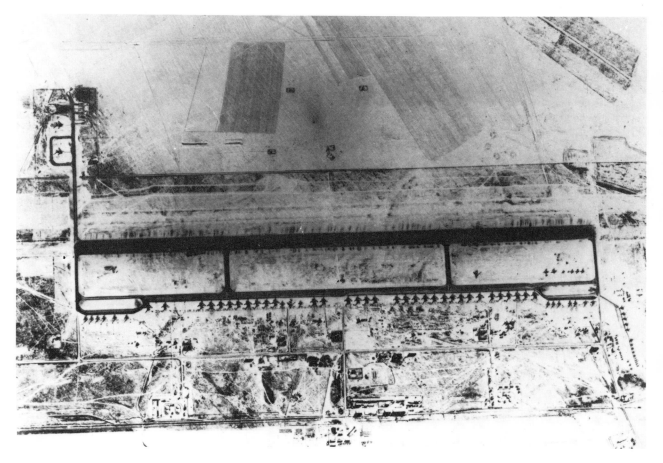

back to WW2 when Soviet industry moved eastwards to escape the Nazi invasion. During the Cold War the accuracy of maps and target intelligence held by the US Air Force and the British Royal Air Force left a lot to be desired; with only limited intelligence coming from agents in the field and other sources, large gaps remained in their knowledge of Soviet industrial and military capability. Stand-off aerial reconnaissance of peripheral targets was one answer, but the vastness of the Soviet Union left only one option, given the state of the art at that time—overflight.

In the early days this snooping operation fell to the de Havilland Mosquito PR.34s of the Royal Air Force. One of the units concerned was No 540 Sqn,

LEFT
The de Havilland Mosquito PR.34 was an extremely capable long-range reconnaissance aircraft. Powered by two-stage Merlin 114s, PR.34s were stripped of all armour to stretch their service ceiling by 3,000 ft (914 m), but on the debit side speed was reduced to 250 mph (463 km/h) carrying two 200 Imp gal (909 lit) drop tanks (Peter Randall)

A mix of US Air Force and Royal Air Force crews stand in front of four Martin RB-45E Tornados of the 91st Strategic Reconnaissance Group (SRG) at RAF Sculthorpe in the early 1950s. Despite their prominent RAF markings the Tornados remained US government property; false serial numbers were applied under the tail section

based at RAF Benson in Oxfordshire. Flying at altitudes in excess of 43,000 ft (13,110 m), immunity from interception by Soviet fighters was virtually guaranteed—Soviet radar technology was still in its infancy just after the war and accurate GCI (ground control of interception) took many years to establish. Reconnaissance flights over such places as Murmansk and Archangel continued until at least 1949.

US Air Force bombers returned to Britain in July 1948 during the Berlin Airlift and less than two years later, in April 1950, a US Navy Privateer with a crew of ten onboard was shot down in the Baltic. In November 1951 a Neptune was downed by MiG-15s near Vladivostok. Between 1949 and 1952, the 5th Strategic Reconnaissance Group (SRG) from Travis AFB operated Boeing RB-29s from RAF Sculthorpe and RAF Burtonwood. Like the Mosquitos, their high-altitude performance and long-range (with the added bonus of greater stability) made them ideal photographic platforms. Electronic intelligence (Elint) was also gathered during these flights.

In January 1951 a small detachment of four RB-45 Tornados from the 91st SRG at Lockbourne AFB in Ohio were observed at RAF Manston in Kent. In February, the Manston-based operation was transferred to Sculthorpe. Later, they were removed from the authority of Strategic Air Command (SAC) and 'loaned' to the RAF. Painted in RAF markings and flown by a mixed crew of US Air Force and RAF personnel, they were used for high-altitude nighttime overflights of the Soviet Union and Warsaw Pact countries for nearly three years. No aircraft were lost during these nocturnal operations, but by 1954 developing Soviet anti-aircraft capability made it prudent to stop using RB-45s for this role. They were transferred to the 19th Tactical Reconnaissance (Night-Photo-Jet) Squadron at Sculthorpe initially under the control of the 3rd Air Force.

Not surprisingly the Soviet Union became increasingly sensitive to Western incursions and carried out a series of attacks on any aircraft suspected of airspace violations. In April 1952 an Air France DC-4 was attacked and damaged in the Berlin Corridor and less than two months later a Swedish Air Force C-47 was downed into the Baltic Sea east of Gotland. A search and rescue PBY was attacked looking for survivors. The Russians meant business. Four months later MiG-15s destroyed a reconnoitering RB-29. On 10 March 1953 a US Air Force F-84 Thunderjet was shot down over Bavaria by Czech MiG-15s. Two days later an RAF Lincoln (RF531) of the Central Gunnery School was shot down in the Berlin Corridor by MiG-15s; seven crew lost their lives. On 15 March 1953 an RB-50 of the 38th SRS, 55th SRW, flown by Lt Col Robert Rich was intercepted by a Soviet MiG-15. The gunner, T/Sgt Jesse Prim, returned fire and the MiG withdrew. But on 29 July another RB-50 from the same wing was not so lucky. Attacked by MiG-15s during a reconnaissance flight near the Soviet border, the RB-50 lost a wing and fell into the Sea of Japan. Co-pilot Capt John E Roche was the only survivor.

Convair RB-36s were also used in the high-altitude strategic reconnaissance role for a short while. One example had a massive 240-inch focal length f8 camera installed in the bomb bay. In August 1954, 18 aircraft from the 5th SRW deployed to RAF Upper Heyford in Oxfordshire on TDY. By 1955, however, SRWs equipped with the RB-36 were redesignated Bombardment Wings and retained only a latent reconnaissance capability.

On 28 October 1956 Israeli paratroopers landed on the West Bank of the Suez Canal, an event which signalled the beginning of the Suez Crisis. British military intervention put the Anglo-American 'special relationship' under extreme pressure, but the RAF had little time to appreciate the political fallout; the Egyptian Air Force had sizable numbers of MiG-15/17 fighters at their disposal, widely dispersed to

Pictured before delivery to No 58 Sqn, BAC Canberra PR.7 WH799 was shot down by a Syrian Air Force Meteor NF.13 when it descended to low-altitude during a reconnaissance mission launched from Akrotiri in Cyprus on 6 November 1956 (British Aerospace)

prevent their destruction on the ground. They posed a real threat to British operations and RAF reconnaissance squadrons were kept busy discovering MiGs and sorting out the real thing from highly convincing dummies. In a rather embarrassing incident which highlighted the shortcomings of existing reconnaissance aircraft, an RAF Canberra PR.7 (WH799) of No 58 Sqn from Akrotiri in Cyprus was shot down by a Syrian Air Force Gloster Meteor NF.13 on the day of the cease fire (6 November 1956). Because of bad weather over the target area, the Canberra descended from 50,000 ft (15,243 m) to 8,000 ft (2439 m) to 'get the pictures'. The navigator was killed, but the pilot, Flt Lt Hunter from No 13 Sqn, and a second pilot were quietly repatriated after behind the scenes diplomatc moves. On 4 October 1957 the Soviet Union launched Sputnik 1 and heralded a more acceptable method of aerial espionage . . .

Following the visit of a CIA-managed Lockheed U-2 to the Royal Aircraft Establishment at Farnborough, Hants, in November 1956, an initial cadre of four RAF pilots (John MacArthur, David Dowling, Michael Bradley, and Christopher Walker) arrived at Laughlin AFB, Texas, to train on the U-2 before operations were conducted from RAF Wat-

ton, Norfolk, with RAF and CIA pilots. RAF Watton also served at this time as the home for No 192 Sqn. This unit's official history describes its role as 'routine radar communications research'. In fact, the unit was the RAF's sole Elint gathering squadron. This unit was equipped with four Canberras, four Comets, a Hastings (for logistic support) and a Varsity; the latter was used to train signals specialists and flew along the east-west German border on flights code named 'Baby Crawl'. This nomadic unit regularly operated detachments from Bodo and Andoye in Norway, Laarbrüch, in West Germany; Teheran in Iran; Akrotiri in Cyprus; Malta, Gibralta and Changi. Obliquely referred to as radio proving flights, data was conveyed to General Communications Headquarters (GCHQ) at Cheltenham in Gloucestershire.

To gather the signal characteristics of Soviet ground and airborne radar, the unit's Canberras were equipped with an unsatisfactory wire recorder unit, switched on by the signaller when a particular signal was intercepted. The recording wire inevitably broke just when it was needed. By the time a replacement wire was fitted the long searched for signal had been switched off. This recorder system was later replaced by a highly reliable 14-channel tape which was carried in the bomb bay.

Flights from Watton would often be made into the Baltic area—a rich hunting ground—usually employing a hi-lo-hi mission profile. Transiting the Baltic Sea in complete radio silence at nearly 35,000 ft (10, 670 m), 'Blue Shadow' sideways looking airborne radar (SLAR) was used to obtain an exact fix of the Canberra's position well before entering the operational area. This active radar unit would then be switched-off to reduce the possibility of detection by triangulation methods.

Navigation would then be conducted using 'Green Satin', a Doppler navigation aid. This system was not without its problems and often became uncoupled in calm sea conditions—leading to difficulties in determining the aircraft's exact position and a

No 51 Sqn based at RAF Wyton in Cambridgeshire, England, specialize in electronic intelligence (Elint), equipped with three British Aerospace Nimrod R.1s. XW664 looks immaculate in the original white/light grey gloss finish also used by the MR.1 anti-submarine version. The entire Nimrod fleet is now painted in light brown 'hemp' camouflage and fitted with wingtip Loral ESM pods
(Robert Cooper)

commensurate inaccurate baseline for successful triangulation of Soviet radar positions. Approaching Gotland the aircraft would let down, simulating to Soviet radar operators an intent to land in Sweden. Once 'behind' the island, the pilot would continue to descend to 500 ft (152 m) or lower and then proceed north, below Soviet radar cover, before turning east and finally climbing on a southerly heading in international airspace off the Soviet coast. These deceptive movements tried to catch the defences off guard, obtaining signal information before any new devices were switched off. On 1 August 1958 the unit was redesignated No 51 Sqn and five years later moved to its present base at RAF Wyton. Today the unit carries out much the same task flying specially equipped Nimrods R.1s.

The 55th SRW based at Forbes AFB, Kansas, carried out similar missions. In June 1954 the unit began trading-in their RB-50s for RB-47s. On 1 July 1960, an RB-47H on detachment from that unit took off from RAF Brize Norton. Tasked with an Elint mission over the Barents Sea, it was attacked and shot down by Soviet fighters when it penetrated Soviet airspace. Lt Dean B Phillips, Capt Eugene E Posa, Lt Oscar L Gosforth were killed; Capts Freeman B Olmstead and John R McKone were picked up and imprisoned for six months in Moscow before being returned to the United States. In addition, the body of the pilot Maj Willard Palm was recovered from a raft in Soviet territorial waters and returned to the USA.

In November 1960 the 55th was in the thick of it again. Its RB-47s started Elint and Photint coverage of an island which became the focus of a major east-west confrontation. On 2 August 1962 a CIA U-2 obtained the first photographs which confirmed the belief of a Soviet military buildup in Cuba. Some weeks later, on 14 October 1962, a CIA U-2 flown by Maj Heyser of the US Air Force brought back photographs showing medium range ballistic missile (MRBM) sites under construction on the island of Cuba. Their proximity to mainland America caused a storm of protest. Political dialogue between Kennedy and Khruschchev was underlined by US military posturing, which included a naval blockade and intense air activity calculated to secure the removal of these weapons from the island. On 27 October, during one of the now daily U-2 overflights of Cuba, Maj Rudolph Anderson was shot down by an SA-2.

On 28 October, the Soviet Government agreed to dismantle all offensive missile sites on Cuba. The Soviet Union also guaranteed not to re-introduce any offensive weapons to Cuba. A treaty for the Prohibition of Nuclear Weapons in Latin America was signed at Tlatelolco, Mexico, by representatives of 21 Latin American countries on 14 February 1967. A major stumbling block was 'Additional Protocol II', in which the nuclear powers (USA, USSR, Britain, France and China) were requested to respect 'the status of denuclearization of Latin America' and to undertake 'not to use or threaten to use nuclear weapons' against contracting parties of the treaty. In the absence of signature and ratification by Cuba and Guyana, this treaty remains in abeyance. Close monitoring of Cuban military capability continues.

The 7406th Combat Support Squadron operated C-130A-IIs and C-130B-IIs from Rhein-Main in West Germany on Comint flights. On 2 September 1958 a C-130 A-II from this unit, on TDY at Incirlik, Turkey, was shot down on a flight to 'study radio wave propagation from US radio stations'. The aircraft crashed 30 miles (55 km) north of Yerevan in Soviet Armenia, killing six of its crew of seventeen. The fate of the surviving crew members is still unknown.

RIGHT
The U-2. 56-6701 led an active service career, starting out as a U-2A (pictured) and subsequently upgraded into a U-2B and finally a U-2C before it was presented to the SAC museum at Offutt AFB, Nebraska, wearing a black paint scheme
(Lockheed-California)

The U-2 thirty years on. Now in much-modified TR-1 guise, the aircraft is used in the tactical-reconnaissance role, 10 examples from the total buy of 24 being equipped with the precision location/strike system (PLSS). Two TR-1B two-seat trainers have been delivered
(Lockheed-California)

Another unit of interest that visited Rhein-Main was the 4028th SRS. Equipped with RB-57s, these high flying aircraft mainly acquired photographic reconnaissance. One aircraft (53-3963) was equipped to obtain radar pictures using a nose mounted AN/ANP-107 and APQ-56 SLAR system located in a fuselage mounted fairing. From 1959 to mid-1964 these tasks were performed by the 7407th Support Squadron. Also based at Rhein-Main, their six RB-57Ds gathered reconnaissance during peripheral flights in 'Operation Bordertown'. A number of RB-57Ds were later made available to the Chinese Nationalist Air Force. On 7 October 1959 one such aircraft was returning to its base at Taoyuan, to the north of Taiwan, after a reconnaissance sortie over Communist China. The pilot commenced his let down from altitude rather earlier than necessary and was shot down by Chinese air defences. In September 1962 the first of several CIA U-2s acquired by the Nationalist Chinese Air Force to replace the vulnerable RB-57s was shot down near Nanching in Communist China.

On 28 January 1964 a US Air Force T-39 on a routine training flight over Germany became hopelessly lost and strayed behind the border. The airplane was shot down and all three crew members died. As a direct result of this disaster, the 'Brass Monkey' call was devised. Radar controllers in West Germany would broadcast 'Brass Monkey, Brass Monkey, Brass Monkey; turn west immediately' to any aircraft which looked as if it might inadvertently penetrate the buffer zone. Despite this, on 10 March 1964, an RB-66C of the 10th Tactical Reconnaissance Wing, based at Touls-Rosires in France, was shot down 15 miles (27 km) behind the East German border near Gardelegen; only two crew members ejected safely. This aircraft may have been lured behind the border by Soviet deception. Navigating with reference to the radio facility at Gutersloh, the crew could have received false radio bearings from a second beacon operating on a similar frequency inside East Germany. To investigate this 'meconing' method, a Canberra from No 51 Sqn was directed by an Air Ministry order to fly several sorties code-named 'Sun'. The precise results of that study remain classified.

On 27 April 1965 during an Elint gathering flight off the coast of Korea, an RB-47 of the 55th SRW was attacked by two North Korean MiGs. A furious gun battle saw two of the RB-47s engines knocked out and a third damaged. Hydraulic lines and major systems were also badly shot-up, but with great flying skill and the use of the aircraft's twin 20 mm cannon, Lt Col Hobert D Mattisen and co-pilot 1/Lt Henry E Dubury managed to disengage and limp back to Yokota AB, Japan. A successful recovery revealed the extensive damage inflicted during the attack. The aircraft was scrapped.

On 27 January 1967 the 55th SRW received its first RC-135 which flew its first operational flight on 1 April in the same year. The full transition from RB-47s to the new RC-135s was completed on 29 December 1967. In addition to the vital work of electronic surveillance of radar equipment and Comint, a small number of RC-135s have also monitored Soviet ICBM performance as the missiles re-enter the Earth's atmosphere heading for the range on the Kamachatka peninsular, north of Japan. Originally part of the 'Rivet' programme, the title was later switched to 'Cobra'. Flown by the 24th SRS, based at Eielson AFB Alaska, the unit detached

LEFT
Operated by SAC, each RC-135 is staffed by between 15 and 20 linguists and signal specialists from Electronic Security Command (ESC) to monitor and interpret significant electronic, signal, communication, and telemetry data. RC-135s can remain airborne for over 12 hours with inflight refuelling
(LeRoy D Nielsen)

Three Boeing RC-135Cs (63-9792, 64-14847, and 64-14849) were converted to RC-135U configuaration during 1970–71. Pictured at RAF Mildenhall on 1 September 1976, this aircraft is either RC-135U '14847 or '14849—the serial number 14850 on the nose and tail is bogus
(Robin A Walker)

aircraft for these, and other monitoring operations in the area, to the island of Shemya in the Aleutian Islands. The telemetry intelligence (Telint) data gathered over the years has been of vital importance, revealing general missile performance, accuracy, and the number of re-entry vehicles (RVs) carried by Soviet missiles.

By 1952 it had become apparent that converted bombers were easy prey for defending fighters over Soviet territory. During the closing months of that year Maj John Seaberg, then Assistant Chief of New Developments, Bombardment Branch, at Wright Field in Ohio, re-defined contemporary high-altitude strategic reconnaissance philosophy. An operational requirement had yet to be written, and on 27 March 1952 Seaberg completed a general design specification and proposed work statement for a special reconnaissance aircraft weapon system. By January 1954 the three companies approached by Seaberg and his superior, William Lamar, had returned their studies to Wright Field for evaluation. A classified project, designated MX-2147 and code named 'Bald Eagle' favoured new Fairchild M-195 and Bell Model 67 designs over the improved B-57 proposal from Martin. But following briefings by Seaberg to Air Research and Development Command (ARDC), SAC, and finally Air Force Headquarters, immediate approval was given to press ahead with the B-57D programme as a stop-gap while further design studies were conducted on the Bell proposal.

By May 1954 a fourth company had become involved in 'Bald Eagle'. An unsolicited proposal by Clarence L Johnson, advanced design bureau chief of Lockheed's Advanced Design Projects (ADP) arrived at Wright Field. ADP acquired the name 'Skunk Works' from the *Al Capp 'Li'l Abner'* newspaper comic strip when 'Kelly' Johnson built the first unit of his highly specialized and secret manufacturing plant near Lockheed's plastics shop. The odour from this proved too much for Ervin Culver, a talented engineer on Johnson's team who later invented the rigid rotor system for helicopters. Culver answered the telephone by identifying the facility as the 'Skunk Works' (after Hairless Joe's foul smelling Dogpatch Kickapoo Joy Juice factory). The name stuck. Johnson—who had designed such aircraft as the P-38, F-80, Constellation and F-104—was highly respected inside the upper echelons of United States military aviation; it was inevitable that he would be 'in' on the work progressing at Wright Field.

Johnson's proposal (Lockheed Report No 9732) was designated the CL-282 and consisted of a slightly modified XF-104 fuselage and tail section with a large span, high aspect-ration wing. Originally powered by a General Electric J73-GE-3 non-afterburning turbojet, this was later revised and the design changed significantly to incorporate the more powerful Pratt and Whitney J57 engine. The Killian Committee set up by the Department of Defense

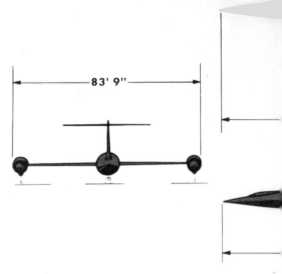

CL-400 GENERAL AR

T.O.G.W.	69,955 LB.
ZERO F.W.	48,515 LB.
FUEL LOAD	21,440 LB.
PAYLOAD	1,500 LB.
CREW	2
WING AREA	2,400 SQ.FT.
ASPECT RATIO	2.5
304-2 ENGINES	TWO

83' 9"

(DoD) to examine military planning and weapons developments on a global scale, were introduced to 'Bald Eagle' and delivered its recommendations to Secretary of Defense, Charles Wilson, and Allen Dulles, Director of the CIA, in November 1954. They all favoured the Lockheed design and decided to brief President Eisenhower. He agreed that funding and direction for the CL-282 project, code-named 'Aquatone', should be controlled by the CIA. Air Force money would be used to purchase the special J57 engines. The Bell 67, now designated X-16 by the Air Force (as a cover) would also be developed under Air Force or 'blue suit' direction and funding. Twenty B-57s were to be modified in accordance with earlier proposals while these new untried designs were being developed.

Concerned about the possible reaction of the Soviet Union to CIA U-2s overflying their airspace, President Eisenhower proposed an 'Open Skies' plan at the Geneva Summit on 21 July 1955. Participating countries would submit to a limited number of annual reconnaissance overflights to allow verification of their military strength, thereby 'easing the

GEMENT

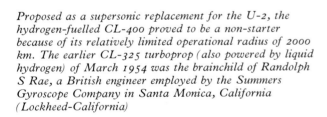

Proposed as a supersonic replacement for the U-2, the hydrogen-fuelled CL-400 proved to be a non-starter because of its relatively limited operational radius of 2000 km. The earlier CL-325 turboprop (also powered by liquid hydrogen) of March 1954 was the brainchild of Randolph S Rae, a British engineer employed by the Summers Gyroscope Company in Santa Monica, California (Lockheed-California)

Ben Rich was closely involved with the CL-400 project before he began work on the first 'Blackbird'—the A-12. Now President of the Lockheed Advanced Aeronautics Company, he is a key figure in the Stealth programme (Lockheed-California)

fear of war in the anxious hearts of people everywhere'. Although approved one month later by a majority of the United Nations, Khruschev remained deeply suspicious of the West and refused to commit the Soviet Union to such a proposal. Without a positive undertaking from this superpower, 'Open Skies' was a non-starter which succumbed shortly afterwards.

The Lockheed CL-282 (now designated U-2) first flew on 1 August 1955 after an inadvertent hop the day before. During a series of briefings it was decided that the 'Agency' should handle the high-altitude reconnaissance programme. Accordingly, the Bell X-16 was cancelled in October 1955.

On 4 July 1956, Lockheed U-2 airframe (article number) 347, serial 56-6680, conducted the first overflight of the Soviet Union and landed at Weisbaden in West Germany. In total approximately 30 overflights and innumerable peripheral flights were flown before the Powers incident.

Never one to rest upon the fruits of success, Kelly Johnson believed the Soviets would develop improved radar and missiles that would render his 'U-bird' vulnerable to attack within two years. Having gained experience during a three month contract with the Garrett Corporation, studying hydrogen-fuelled aircraft in 1955, he submitted a proposal for a supersonic follow-on to the U-2. In the Pentagon, any proposal that would restore some Air Force pride in the wake of the realignment of 'Bald Eagle' was bound to generate a great deal of interest. Johnson met Lt Gen Donald L Putt, deputy Chief of Staff for development and offered to build two prototype hydrogen-fuelled aircraft, the first of which would fly within 18 months. Flying at 99,500 ft (30, 335 m) the CL-400 would cruise at Mach 2.5 and have a range of 2,500 miles (4630 km). It was a tempting proposal for the Air Force. By 20 February 1956, a feasibility study into powerplant design had been held between the General Electric Company and Pratt & Whitney. The latter won, and on 1 May a fixed cost, six month contract was signed. Agreement was also reached with Lockheed who held out for a provisional contract that could be renegotiated and repriced at the end of six months. This highly classified project, code-named 'Suntan', was access-limited to such a degree that only about 25 people knew of the full research and development effort.

In order to achieve the tight development timeframe of two or three years and maintain security by reducing paperwork, the authorities granted waivers to the 'Suntan' team which allowed them to award contracts directly with a minimum of review. Ben Rich, Kelly Johnson's protege and a brilliant thermodynamist, was responsible for propulsion and hydrogen-handling design. He and his Skunk Works team had to master handling far greater quantities of liquid hydrogen than ever before. Despite the highly temperamental nature of liquid hydrogen not a single accident occurred. Distinguished guests visiting the plant were extremely impressed with what they saw, and their tour was often concluded with 'Martini-icicles'. A gin and vermouth mixture was poured into a paper cup, a lollypop stick inserted, and the complete ensemble immersed in liquid hydrogen. The result was a frozen Martini on a stick.

During this six month development period, it became apparent to Johnson that the best achievable radius of action would only be in order of 2000 km. The Air Force continued to insist on a minimum radius of 2800 km. Stretching the fuselage to increase fuel capacity would only result in a 3 per cent increase in range. Pratt & Whitney estimated that no better than a 5–6 per cent improvement in specific fuel consumption (SFC) could be achieved by their '304' engine over a five year period of operation. This low growth potential coupled with the logistical problems of pre-positioning liquid hydrogen at overseas locations convinced Johnson that the airplane was a non-starter. When Johnson informed Secretary of the Air Force James H Douglas Jr it caused gloom among the hydrogen-propulsion planners. Thereafter, the 'Suntan' slowly faded and funds were progressively reduced. The programme was eventually cancelled in February 1959 when the two prototypes were almost complete.

Kelly Johnson turned his attention to designing an airplane powered by hydrocarbon fuel. A derivative of this design would stay at the forefront of aviation achievement for over 20 years.

Chapter 1
Oxcart and the A-12

Between 21 April 1958 and 1 September 1959, Kelly Johnson submitted a series of unsolicited proposals for a manned aircraft capable of global reconaissance missions at speeds in excess of Mach 3 to Richard Bissell of the CIA, and the US Air Force. This series of U-2 replacement aircraft carried Skunk Works' design numbers A-1 through A-12 and were in competition with design submissions from Convair and the US Navy.

An in-house US Navy proposal was a unique ramjet-powered, rubber inflatable craft carried aloft by a balloon, then rocket boosted to a speed where ramjets would supply the necessary thrust. With a proposed wing area of a 1/7th of an acre, Lockheed calculated that the carrying balloon would need to be a mile in diameter to lift the unit to ramjet altitude. Not surprisingly, the design proved to be totally useless.

Convair's less exotic challenge was the 'King-fisher', which envisioned a Marquardt ramjet-powered aircraft capable of Mach 4 launched from a B-58. Two flaws arose in this design. First was the inability of the B-58 to reach the required supersonic launch speed with the aircraft in place; and second, this type of powerplant could not operate over a large speed range, increasing the probability of a ramjet blow-out during certain manoeuvres.

On 29 August 1959, Lockheed's A-12 design was declared the winner and Dick Bissell gave the company four months to build a full-scale mockup and conduct further proof-of-concept testing.

Louis W Schalk, Lockheed's chief test pilot, was to head the flight test team and joined the programme late in 1959. With Dan Zeek, his first task was to help design the cockpit layout; a start had already been made but the design did not conform to the needs of the military or test flying. The programme received a boost on 30 January 1960 when the 'Agency' gave Lockheed the go-ahead to manufacture and test twelve A-12s, including one two-seat conversion trainer.

Activity amongst Skunk Works engineers increased steadily now as each specialist worked long hours to transform Kelly Johnson's masterful design into a reality. Dave Robertson's responsibility was the fuel system. Henry Combs was in charge of structures, with Dick Baymee as his right-hand man; while Ed Martin was in overall charge of these and many other experienced engineers.

Much use was made of the NACA computer facility at Moffett Field, which was made available after office hours. From that advanced computer, it was discovered that the design had some variability in its speed parameters. Other work carried out during these night simulations by a department which included Dick Fuller, Ben Rich and Burt McMasters, also provided accurate predictive data on flight characteristics. During the summer of 1960, Lou Schalk was able to use some of this information to write a basic aircraft operating handbook. Refinements, ammendments, and additions to the handbook would become available as the flight test programme progressed. To help prepare himself for the first flight in this experimental titanium aircraft, Lou Schalk made three or four flights in NACA's variable stability F-100. By running the centre of gravity (CG) aft, the airplane became very unstable during the simulation of certain predictive flight characteristics of the A-12.

With aircraft construction well underway at the Skunk Works, pilots who were to fly the A-12 took trips to Worchester, Mass., to be outfitted with their personal full pressure suits—identical to those worn by astronauts in the Mercury and Gemini space programmes. Their visits were timed to ensure isolation from the astronauts to preserve security.

High-speed and low-speed wind tunnel tests continued to be run on various A-12 configurations, while a number of full-scale tests were conducted on various structural components. One example was a

full-sized engine nacelle, constructed and fitted with inlet and exhaust plugs. Compressed air was pumped into the test unit to pressures in excess of 50 psi to measure air leakage from the inlet system. Attention to proper sealing during inlet construction reduced drag-inducing nacelle air leakage.

LEFT
Louis W Schalk was the first man to fly the A-12—the proof-of-concept vehicle which eventuated as the SR-71 Blackbird. Pictured just before he left the F-104 flight test team to join 'Oxcart', Schalk poses in front of Speedy, *the Starfighter which set a new absolute airspeed record of 1,404.19 mph (2260.74 km/h) on 16 May 1958 (Lockheed-California)*

Eight A-12s and two YF-12s (background) lined up at Groom Lake, Nevada, during the flight test programme in 1963. The nearest aircraft is the prototype A-12 60-6924 which first flew on 26 April 1962; behind it is the two-seat trainer, 60-6927. All of the aircraft are painted matt black with natural metal upper surfaces (CIA via John Andrews)

No matter how many mathematical models, simulations, and wind tunnel experiments are conducted during design and mockup work, the acid test of any aircraft design is the flight test programme itself. By December 1961 the prototype A-12 was nearly complete. The programme was now code-named 'Oxcart'. During mid-January the prototype, Lockheed article number 121, serial number 60-6924, was moved to Area 53—Groom Lake. Situated in the desert beyond the Sierra Nevada mountains, this highly secret flight research establishment is near to an Atomic Energy Commission nuclear weapons test site, and was founded for testing the U-2 in the early 1950s. Located about 100 miles (185 km) northwest of Las Vegas, just south of Bald Mountain, Nevada, the site offered an expansive dry lake bed and exceptional remoteness. Obliquely referred to as 'The Ranch' or 'The Area', the site and its living facilities were summed up by one Agency pilot as 'desert, windy and hot, windy and cold, isolated, basic'.

The new A-12 was transported in large sections by two specially constructed covered trailers, each

pulled by the biggest Kenworth truck that Lockheed could buy. The slow convoy left Burbank at 3 am in the morning, escorted by the Californian Highway Patrol. By daybreak the convoy was well out on the high desert, away from the view of curious onlookers. On arrival at Groom Lake, the aircraft was reassembled and prepared for its first flight.

The gestation period for developing aero-engines usually exceeds airframe design and construction. The J58 powerplant for the A-12 was no exception. Until these high-thrust engines became available, the aircraft would be powered by the weaker but proven J75.

By 24 April engine test-runs and low/medium-speed taxi tests were completed. It was time for Lou Schalk to take the aircraft on a high-speed taxi run that would culminate in a momentary lift-off and landing to roll out into the salt lake bed. For this first test the stability augmentation system (SAS) was left

uncoupled until it could be properly tested in flight. As '121' accelerated down the runway, Lou Schalk remembers *'it all went like a dream, until I lifted off. Thereupon between the lateral directional and longitudinal oscillations, I really didn't think that I was going to be able to sit the aircraft back down on the ground safely. The aircraft was very difficult to handle and I think I became a bit frightened. I finally caught up with everything that was happening, got control back enough to set it back down and chop the power. Touchdown was on the lake bed, not the end of the runway, which created a tremendous cloud of dust into which I disappeared entirely. They were calling me from the tower to find out what was happening. I was answering, but with the UHF antenna located on the underside of the aircraft for best transmittion in flight no one could hear me. Finally, when I slowed down and started my turn on the lake bed, re-emerging from the dust cloud, everyone breathed a huge sigh of relief'.* That night Johnson asked Schalk if the aircraft ought to fly again the next day. The chief pilot thought it should fly adding, *'But I also think we ought to turn the dampers [SAS] on'.*

The first real flight was, in fact, made two days later on 26 April 1962. This trouble-free flight lasted 35 minutes, with the gear left extended to avoid 'historic

The great man himself. 'Kelly' Johnson beams behind his oxygen mask in the raised cockpit of A-12 60-6927, the two-seat trainer, after a faultless flight with test pilot Lou Schalk in 1963. The ejection seat is a Lockheed C-2 (Lockheed-California)

first-flight gear retraction problems'. The SAS performed admirably, with no repetition of the 'bucking bronco ride' experienced two days earlier, as first one, and eventually all three axes of stability dampers were switched off. With all three dampers of the SAS engaged, Schalk terminated the first true A-12 flight with an uneventful landing.

As the landing gear was neatly tucked away on the second flight and 121 began accelerating, panels started peeling off the fuselage and wing fillets. A somewhat anxious chase pilot described the incident as 'shucking corn'. In the cockpit of the A-12 no adverse handling effects were noted, but prudence dictated an early termination of the flight. On the ground it was discovered that several panels were developing inverse pressure areas which were ripping panels off the aircraft. As an interim measure, armament tape was used as a sealant.

Lou Schalk was contracted to fly the first 12 experimental test flights in the A-12, when the all-important SAS was thoroughly checked out at subsonic speeds. An element of superstition led him to also fly the 13th flight on the aircraft; the burden of test flying was then shared with William C Park. Another Lockheed test pilot, James D Eastham, entered the programme in the summer of 1962 and these three pilots began building up flight time on the aircraft. Early systems testing was devoted to various sensors and to the inertial navigation system (INS). Some stability and control tests were also carried out, but little in the way of hardcore high-speed performance data was gathered because the aircraft was still equipped with J75 engines. A third prototype was soon added, article number 123, but the second aircraft, 122, had still to be delivered for initial static testing. Another milestone was reached when the first air-refuelling flight was successfully carried out. Tanker support and air-refuelling trials for this clandestine project was provided by the 903rd Air Refuelling Squadron. In return for this essential service, this unit enjoyed an enviable supply priority for their slightly modified KC-135Q tankers.

Time slipped by and there was still no sign of the J58 engines. Agency officials became impatient for some return on their multi-million dollar propulsion investment. The Agency decided that the A-12 should be capable of Mach 2.0 with its current powerplants. They argued that if the J75-powered F-106 could fly at Mach 2.0, why not the A-12? They did not appreciate that the A-12 had been designed to house a pair of J58s; with J75s a penalizing mis-match between the inlet systems and the engine produced inlet airflow vibration, or 'duct shudder' as Mach 2.0 was approached. Finally, in order to placate the directors who controlled the purse strings, Bill Park dived an A-12 to Mach 2.0 and relieved some of the high-level pressure on the design team.

In July 1962 the J58 successfully completed its Pre-Flight Rating Test and in January 1963 the first engine was delivered to Area 53 and installed in aircraft number 1, article 121. This was not accomplished without the usual crop of problems. One early hiccup was ignition—the engine would not start! The small inlet wind tunnel model did not indicate the mass flow of the J58. Indeed, the engine's appetite for air was so big that instead of air flowing out of the compresser's fourth stage bleed ducts, flow reversal occurred, drawing air into the compressor from the back end. As a temporary fix, Lockheed removed an inlet access panel to facilitate ground starts. They subsequently cut holes into the rear section of the nacelle and installed two sets of suck-in doors, while Pratt & Whitney added an engine bleed to the nacelle to improve airflow through the engine during ground starting. Article 121 flew for several months with a J75 in one nacelle and a J58 in the other until confidence in the new engine increased.

In February 1963 the first duty pilot, William L Skliar, joined Oxcart. An outstanding US Air Force test pilot from the Armament Development Center at Eglin AFB, he joined the Agency, like those who were to follow, on a suspended Air Force contract. In common with astronauts on loan to NASA from the services, when Bill Skliar later re-joined the Air Force, a 'review' of his service records would indicate uninterrupted Air Force service during his spell with the Agency. To prepare him and other operational pilots to fly the A-12, a two-seat conversion trainer (article 124) was built. Delivered to Area 53 in late 1962, 60-6927, nicknamed the 'Titanium Goose' was powered throughout its working life by two J75 engines, giving it a crusing speed of somewhat less than Mach 2.0. After a few flights in the two-seat Goose and the completion of a flight check ride, Bill Skliar's task was to evaluate the aircraft for operational suitability and reliability, and to conduct Category II flight tests.

At this stage in the programme a flight was set up for Kelly Johnson in the A-12 to give him a feel for the aircraft's early performance. Lou Schalk was the 'instructor pilot' in the Goose and recalls, '*I took the airplane off, cleaned it up and 'gave it' to Kelly. He climbed the airplane, levelled off with the afterburners in and accelerated out to Mach 1.4. That was the first time he had ever been supersonic and he was delighted.*

'*The airplane behaved beautifully as we proceeded to take an INS trip to one of our check points on the course. I rolled the airplane into a steep bank and there was the check point—a city down in Utah, right on the money. I then contacted the tanker for a refuelling rendezvous— which at times could be a bit 'hit and miss'. He answered my call immediately and was right where he said he was. I picked him out, slid right into position and the boom operator, who was red hot that day, plugged me off and we'd taken on 5,000 lb (2273 kg) of fuel and were gone again before we hardly knew what had happened.*

'*Maybe it wasn't a good idea to have such a good flight with the Boss, to whom you were supposed to impress with all the problems that you were having, but it was a beautiful flight and I'm sure glad he was there*'.

Test aircraft were heavily instrumented to accumulate in flight data. A 35 mm camera system, referred to as the Automatic Observer (AO), was located in the 'Q' bay behind the pilot. Within this compartment a cluster of gauges supplied a near-complete record of flight and engine parameters, including fuel consumption, centre of gravity location, etc. Despite compartment cooling, high temperatures dictated that a 400 ft (122 m) roll of new film be loaded for each test flight, no matter how much was used, to minimize the culmulative effects of heat on the film emulsion. In addition, a multi-channel oscillograph provided strain guage signals so that airframe flight loads could be related to stress in various parts of the structure, while a 'Brown' temperature recorder gathered airframe data through a large number of thermocouple inputs.

When a second J58 engine was installed in article 121 the flight-test programme expanded. Development of the J58 increased thrust from 29,000 up to 32,500 lb (13,182–14,742 kg) before the line finally closed. As the envelope extension programme slowly began to edge up the aircraft's top speed, other problems were highlighted. Initial flight results with the airplane in this new configuration were not at all encouraging for Lou Schalk, and he confided in Bill Park, who had chased him in an F-104. '*Look Bill you're going to fly this airplane pretty soon, but don't say too much about how bad it accelerates, we're never gonna make Mach 3. But let's not get this programme cancelled 'til someone figures out how to make this thing run right*'. After Park flew the aircraft with the two J58s he said, '*Lou, you're right, but let's keep this under our hats*'. Perhaps the two test pilots were joking, but there was certainly cause for concern.

Heavy wear and cracks on the long drive shafts between the engine and its remote gearbox became a problem along with twisting and heavy spline wear. This was caused by a four-inch displacement of the gearbox relative to the engine during High-Mach transients. A double universal joint on a new shaft between the two components solved the problem. In addition, the aircraft's fuel system ahead of the engine showed signs of fatigue and distortion. Measurements from a fast recorder showed that pressure levels at the engine fuel inlet were going off the scale. This overpressuring was caused by feed-back from the engine hydraulic system. The phenomenon had failed to materialize in rig tests and during engine ground testing because large fluid volumes were not involved.

The Skunk Works invented a 'high temperature sponge'—promptly named the football—to be in-

stalled ahead of the engines for reducing pressure levels to more tolerable figures. Certain manoeuvers resulted in engine plumbing being crushed, as the outer half of the nacelle rotated into the engine. Pratt & Whitney redesigned the rear engine mounting and incorporated a tangential link between the underside of the engine and the outboard side of the nacelle. A finite distance was thereby always maintained between engine and nacelle. Another related problem with the exhaust ejector nozzle concerned an unacceptably high fuel consumption when going transonic. Test instrumentation recorded inflight thrust measurements, Mach number, and ejector operation. It was discovered that the ejector went

The only photograph released by the US Air Force of a single-seat 'Agency' A-12 in flight; 60-6932 was lost as a result of a technical malfunction during an operational mission from Kadena, Japan, on 5 June 1968, killing CIA pilot Jack Weeks (Lockheed-California)

supersonic long before the aircraft. The problem rectified itself when one of the test pilots went transonic at lower altitude and raised the equivalent airspeed datum from 350 to 400 knots (648–741 km/h).

As greater speeds and altitudes were attained cockpit cooling began to cause problems. Park recalls that the control stick got so hot he had to change hands regularly to keep hold of it. Temperatures got so high in the upper areas of the cockpit that they blackened 130° templates placed on the pilots helmets. By redirecting the incoming flow from the AiResearch air conditioning unit and employing a special bootstrap cooling unit, Lockheed eventually provided a tolerable cockpit environment.

The biggest problem was the air induction system, designed to help propel the aircraft at its intended sustained cruise speed of Mach 3.2. To achieve this augmented thrust, the inlet spike schedule had to be programmed accurately. When that was achieved, the airplane's thirst for fuel considerably decreased. In all it took 66 flights to push the speed envelope out from Mach 2.0 to Mach 3.2. Such flights from Groom Lake tread a well worn path to the north over Wendover, Utah, and then up to the Canadian border, where a 180° turn would be executed. During the return leg home between 65–72,000 ft (19,817–21,951 m), the aircraft would reach its test

point. The progression to higher speeds (accomplished in tenth-of-a-Mach-number increments) would be achieved whilst heading back to 'The Ranch', simplifying aircraft recovery in the event of an emergency. Early in the programme the callsign 'Asteroid' was used. Later, it changed to 'Dutch' and a two figure number, giving each pilot a personalized callsign throughout his time with the programme. In addition a pool of five McDonnell F-101B and two Lockheed F-104 chase aircraft were provided for the subsonic and transonic phases of the flight.

Cockpit workload during the early test programme was extremely high, since the turbine inlet temperature (TIT) tended to wander. This variation needed close monitoring if engine damage was to be avoided. Flying at 100 per cent rpm, unstable TITs caused thrust variations. Two toggle switches—one for each engine—were introduced to allow the pilot to trim the fuel flow manually without adjusting the throttles to maintain the TIT within limits. Two rotating wafer switches controlled the inlet spike position, while a third set of switches controlled the bypass door positions. Flying the aircraft and manually operating six control switches, while determining the optimum inlet schedule, would have been practically impossible during unstable flight without the Minneapolis-Honeywell SAS. This gyro-stabilized system, coupled into the autopilot made life in the cockpit more tolerable, despite the disheartening effect of persistently using a third of the total fuel load accelerating to speed. The slow early progression out to speed was the result of a trial and error workup of optimum door and spike inlet schedules. When this was completed, the inlet system could be programmed to operate automatically.

During these tests, speed was gently increased by one tenth of a Mach number and the next spike position selected. If all worked well, the aircraft was decelerated and the spike position was analysed in the labs and incorporated into the schedule. More often however, the spike position would not match the inlet duct requirements and a vicious 'unstart' would invariably follow causing harsh yawing movements which swung the nose in the direction of the 'unstarted' engine, bouncing the pilot's head from one side of the canopy to the other 'causing his eyeballs to touch all their limit switches'. To break an unstarted inlet and recapture the disturbed shock wave, the pilot would open the bypass doors on the unstarted engine and slowly return them to the smooth but less efficient position they were in just before the incident. Incessant problems in the air induction system caused Lockheed to change the inlet geometry and to change trim schedules. In addition the manual trim system was speeded up. During that first year the inlet control system was changed often and on many flights the two inlets never seemed to track together—a characteristic that remained with the original control system. Returning from a night training sortie, during which he

experienced innumerable unstarts, one of the Agency pilots walked into the ops building at Groom Lake for debriefing wearing a Beatle wig and cracked 'Man, that was a hairy flight.' Unstarts seemed to typify early A-12 flights.

Thermodynamic considerations had dictated the use of a minimum number of electrical installations in the aircraft. Pneumatic steam pressure gauges were installed on the inlet system to sense pressure variations of less than $\frac{1}{2}$ lb sq inch. Positioning of the translating inlet spike was based on a schedule derived from those pressure readings. After a multitude of inlet malfunctions and unstarts, it became apparent that these instruments were not sensitive enough for the job. Aircraft were coming off the line with the pneumatic system installed, but Kelly Johnson decided that they should be replaced by an electrically controlled system. Manufactured by Garrett, the new system initially required far more maintenance per flight hour than the pneumatic system, but its inflight performance was far superior. Despite the heavy additional cost, the electrical system was retrofitted to existing aircraft and all production aircraft from number nine (60-6932) onwards.

Before the new spike control system was flight tested, many ground electro magnetic induction (EMI) tests were carried out to ensure good integration and non-interfering operation. All was thought to be functioning well until a radio check made the inlet spikes retract. Clearly, a bit more work was still necessary. When Bill Park briefed the operational pilots about the new system, adding that unstarts would soon be almost a thing of the past, he was virtually 'booed off stage'. But once installed the system immediately began to prove its worth and the number of unstarts decreased dramatically; fuel consumption also improved significantly due to tighter inlet spike scheduling.

The first A-12 accident occured on 24 May 1963 when an Agency pilot, Ken Collins, was flying a routine subsonic training mission to test the inertial navigation system (INS) in serial number 60-6926, article 123. Flying above an overcast, he entered clouds and water vapour collected in the pitot static system and froze. Consequently, the airspeed indicator displayed the incorrect airspeed. The

Covered in thermocouples, YF-12A 60-6935 underwent extensive testing at NASA's Dryden Flight Research Centre in the high temperature loads lab. The twin vertical fins have been removed. Quartz heat lamps (pictured in the raised position before being applied to the skin of the aircraft), recreated the temperatures encountered in flight to assist engineers in the development of instrumentation and test procedures for the next generation of high-speed aircraft
(NASA)

airplane stalled and pitched up out of control. The pilot ejected safely from an inverted flat spin.

While flying 60-6924 on an inlet schedule flight, Lou Schalk experienced the most thrilling flight of his distinguished flying career. He said, '*We had the electrically controlled spike by this time. I was approaching Wendover and the aircraft was accelerating like it had never done before. It was apparent that I would be at Mach 3 before I ever left Utah, much less reached the turn point short of the Canadian border; so I throttled back and started my turn early (restricted to 40° bank angles at high speed, a 180° turn has a diameter of approximately 130 miles). Emerging from the turn I reselected full power and continued to climb. I got so far behind the aircraft that I didn't notice that the fuel flow fell off slightly which led to a loss in RPM on one engine.*

An A-12 cockpit section was placed in an oven to study the effects of high temperatures on the structure and electrical systems
(Lockheed-California)

'*The next thing, I got an unstart. I turned the inlet bypass switch to break the unstart, but it didn't seem to help. Then the other engine unstarted and so it went on, with these terrific oscillations continuing, one after another. I made a single radio transmission, to the effect that I was in real trouble and that's all I said for at least five minutes. I thought I ought to bail out, but stayed with the aircraft because it still seemed to be in one piece.*

'*I was experiencing difficulty in decelerating and these violent oscillations continued all the way down to Mach 1.4. I then realised that I'd left the right engine in burner and the left engine had flamed out. I was holding this tremendous rudder pressure with my legs without even trimming it out with a rudder trim switch. I couldn't believe it, but there it was. I came out of afterburner and got the other engine started, then recovered the aeroplane back to home base.*

'*At the debrief I learned that the engineers had decided at their weekly maintenance briefing that the slow acceleration and high fuel consumption could be due to the doors leaking air after they had been closed. They therefore decided to 'bolt' them closed. No one had told me about this and that's why the aircraft had taken off on me like a scorched dog. It also explained why I*

couldn't break the unstart—when I turned the switch to open the bypass doors nothing was happening. Having determined that the bypass doors were not functioning as they should, a simple fix rectified the problem. However, after that I attended all the 7 am Monday morning maintenance planning briefings.'

Today of course, test instrumentation would have highlighted such a problem immediately. Twenty-five years ago however, such developments hadn't kept pace with the kind of advances Kelly Johnson had made in aircraft design.

How would the airframe react to the sustained, high-stagnation temperatures encountered during prolonged heat soaking at high Mach number? A test to answer this question was devised, and called for the aircraft to cruise at Mach 3.16 for precisely 10 minutes. The test procedure was followed exactly as planned after the turn back to Groom Lake, the required speed was reached and maintained. The aircraft decelerated safely and recovered to base. After getting out of article 121, Lou Schalk recalls the senior flight test engineer Glen Fulkerson saying, 'We'll turn it round and fly it tomorrow.' This proved to be wishful thinking.

An inspection revealed that due to an error in the pitot static system, the flight had exceeded Mach 3.2. This higher speed caused stagnation temperatures to rocket upwards, incinerating practically all of the electrical wiring. Additionally, most of the hydraulic fluid activating the flight controls had also disappeared. Ground tests using heat lamps to heat up the rudder servos revealed that at high speed and high temperatures joints in these units opened up. The heat-thinned special dewaxed mineral oil hydraulic fluid, (developed by Pennsylvania State University) leaked instantly. On cooling, the joints closed up again, giving no clue as to where the leaks had occurred. That airplane did not fly again for nearly eight weeks, but during this time wiring was improved and replaced.

Pitot static changes were made to give an accurate Mach indication and a hydraulic quantity indicator added. After one or two maintenance check flights, the aircraft was readied once more for a sustained flight at high Mach number. Test plans were revised to suitably reflect the lessons learned and at first light the aircraft got airborne. During the 30 minute, Mach 3-plus cruise, pilot Jim Eastham also tested various sensors and the communications equipment—all functioned as advertised. On descent, deceleration, and return to the Groom Lake traffic pattern one of the hydraulic systems failed, and the gear had to be blown down. A post-flight inspection revealed that the failure was caused by the brake manufacturuer installing an aluminium plug in the brake damper. High temperatures during the flight had caused the plug to extrude from its hole, leading to a loss of hydraulic activiting fluid. Kelly's comment of the incident was 'how the hell did a piece of aluminium get into this airplane'. It was duly

replaced by a titanium or steel plug.

With the flight test programme progressing well, the Special Activities Squadron at Groom Lake (also known as 'The Roadrunners') trained seven Agency pilots, making up the first cadre who conducted a great deal of sensor testing. All were confident that they had a platform that could carry on from where the U-2 had left off. On 29 February 1964, these pilots were incredulous when President Lyndon B Johnson blew the programme for political prestige in response to a challenge by Senator Barry Goldwater for the Presidency.

'The United States has successfully developed an advanced experimental jet aircraft, the A-11, which has been in sustained flight at more than 2,000 mph and at altitudes in excess of 70,000 ft.

'The performance of the A-11 far exceeds that of any other aircraft in the world today. The development of this aircraft has been made possible by major advances in aircraft technology of great significance to both military and commercial application.

'Several A-11 aircraft are now being flight-tested at Edwards Air Force Base, in California.

'The existence of this programme is being disclosed to permit the orderly exploitation of this advanced technology in our military and commercial planes. This advanced experimental aircraft, capable of high-speed and high-altitude and long-range performance at thousands of miles, constitutes the technological accomplishment that will facilitate the achievement of a number of important military and commercial requirements. The A-11 aircraft now at Edwards Air Force Base are undergoing extensive tests to determine their capabilities as long-range interceptors. The development of supersonic commerical transport aircraft will also be greatly assisted by the lessons learned from this A-11 programme. For example, one of the most important technological achievements in this project has been the mastery of the metalurgy and fabrication of titanium metal which is required for the high temperatures experienced by aircraft travelling at more than three times the speed of sound.

'Arrangements are being made to make this and other important technical developments available under appropriate safeguards to those directly engaged in the supersonic transport programme.

'This project was first started in 1959. Appropriate members of the Senate and House have been kept fully informed on the programme since the day of its inception.

'The Lockheed Aircraft Corporation, at Burbank, California, is the manufacturer of the aircraft. The aircraft engine, the J58 was designed and built by the Pratt & Whitney Aircraft Division, United Aircraft Corp. The experimental fire control and air-to-air missile system for the A-11 was developed by the Hughes Aircraft Corporation'.

In addition to being the first pilot to fly the A-12, Lou Schalk was also the first to take the aircraft to Mach 3 and above 90,000 ft (27,439 m). He was also to have been the first to overfly the USSR. When

Eight A-12s in storage at Palmdale after their retirement in 1968. The two-seat 'Titanium Goose' near the back of the building still has a 'two-tone' paint job (Lockheed-California)

President Johnson revealed the entire programme, he realized that the airplane would not fly the deep penetration sorties into the Soviet Union for which it had originally been designed. Indeed, with the programme behind schedule and the impressive early imagery from satellite-based cameras, there was concern amongst the test force that the programme would be cancelled altogether. With much of the work now finished, Lou Schalk left the programme in June 1964 and his position was filled by Bill Park. Later that same year, Bill Park flew the A-12 on a 10,000 mile (16,090 km) air-refuelled demonstration flight. Taking off at first light the flight lasted 6 hours and completed before lunch. That afternoon, he was airborne again and took the aircraft to its maximum altitude-believed to be 95,000 ft (28,963 m)— although a senior aerodynamicist calculated that the aircraft would reach 126,000 ft (38,415 m) in a zoom climb. During this phase of the programme bonus payments were made by Lockheed to their test pilots. In this way extra money would be paid, by way of a differential, for higher cockpit workloads experienced at design speed compared to more straightforward subsonic check flights. Returning to Groom Lake in 60-6939, Park had just completed a high-Mach check flight in this new aircraft when the flight controls locked up on approach. Despite a valiant attempt to save the airplane, the bank angle and descent rate continued to increase and at 1,500 ft (457 m) in a 45° bank, Park ejected safely before '939 flew into the ground. The date was 9 July 1964.

Drones at the Lake

During the mid-1960s a highly classified and innovative programme which married a two-seat A-12 air-launching a D-21 remotely piloted drone was begun. This 'mother-daughter' combination involved two A-12s, serial numbers 60-6940 and 60-6941. A second crew position was created behind the pilot after modification of the 'Q' bay, while a rear fuselage-mounted pylon on the upper surface carried the drone. The titanium D-21, a Skunk Works creation, was powered by a Marquardt RJ-43-MA-11 ramjet. A Launch Control Officer, in the back seat of the A-12, effected separation of the vehicle from the mothership at its cruise speed, which due to its fixed inlet spike is believed to have been about Mach 3.15. He would then 'pilot' the drone, via a command radio control link to the reconaissance collection area while the A-12 mothership would stand-off at a safe distance.

The clean lines of the D-21, coupled with its speed, would make it a difficult target to track on radar or engage. Once in friendly airspace, a cassette of recorded reconnaissance data would be ejected and recovered, probably by a Hercules or helicopter, using a Mid-Air Recovery System (MARS). The drones reconnaissance equipment would then probably have been destroyed by a small charge before the vehicle was allowed to splash into the ocean.

A number of test flights were conducted using the A-12/D-21 combination and it is believed that Bill Park piloted the mothership on all of them. Launch control duties were split between Ray Torick and Keith Beswick, both of whom were Lockheed employees. Many difficulties and often dangerous problems had to be overcome during the buildup phase which led to actual test launches. On 30 July 1966, Park and Torick climbed aboard 60-6941 on a test flight which included flying the D-21 for the first time with a full fuel load. Also to be tested on this particular flight was a slightly modified launch procedure that would, if successful, enable mission pilots to gain mother-daughter separation more easily. Flying Mach 3 chase in 60-6940, Art Peterson, another experienced Lockheed test pilot, along with Keith Beswick in the back, were to obtain film of the launch for analysis. As Park attained launch speed the drone separated from the mothership as planned.

Pictured at Palmdale in October 1980, these A-12s are cocooned and tethered to protect them from the ravages of open storage. A-12s remained on reserve status until 1968 and were finally retired between October 1976 and June 1977
(John Andrews)

A-12 60-6940 during 'mother-daughter' combination trials with the D-21 reconnaissance drone. The pilot is Bill Park—he narrowly escaped with his life when a D-21 struck the A-12 carrier aircraft (60-6941) during the separation test on 30 July 1966 (Lockheed-California)

TOP
Kelly Johnson personally cancelled the A-12/D-21 programme and an attempt was made to use other launch vehicles. The B-52 was probably safer, but it was subsonic—a large booster rocket had to be strapped to the D-21 to accelerate it to Mach 2-plus where its ramjet became effective. This B-52H is carrying two D-21s (Lockheed-California)

Thereafter everything went terribly wrong as subsequent study of Beswick's remarkable film would later reveal.

The D-21 failed to clear the shockwave. It hit the tail section of '6941 causing the aircraft to enter an accelerated pitch-up—cruising at full power the airplane is almost neutrally stable for minimum trim drag. In this unforgiving corner of the envelope, when pitch rates are exceeded they continue to increase, which invariably leads to a stall or breakup (depending upon airspeed). At Mach 3-plus, the fuselage forebody separated from the rest of the aircraft and tumbled earthwards complete with crew. Inside the cockpit, with their life support pressure suits inflated, Park determined that despite their altitude and speed their chances of survival were better outside. Both he and Torick ejected and made a 'feet wet' landing in the ocean. After sometime, Park was picked up by a helicopter. Both men survived this incredible collision, but tragically Torick drowned before he was brought aboard a US Navy vessel.

Kelly Johnson was desperately upset by the loss of one of his team and personally cancelled the entire A-12/D-21 Programme—despite pleas from many of his engineers that the concept was basically sound and could be made to work.

A D-21 perched on its handling dolly at Davis Monthan AFB in December 1979. Had it gone into service, this Mach 3 drone would have proved difficult to intercept by defending fighters and SAMs (Ben Knowles via Chris Pocock)

Instead, the D-21s were modified to incorporate a less sensitive inlet and were launched from two B-52s of the 4200 Test Wing at Beale. This new operation, believed to have been code-named 'Senior Bowl', produced its own environmental problems. Launched from a slower, lower platform operating in steady state temperatures of −50°C, the D-21 was accelerated to its operational cruise speed and altitude by a giant rocket booster fitted to the underside of the drone which separated from the vehicle at high Mach. The thermodynamic stresses were severe as the D-21 blasted up to its design cruise speed when the ramjet powered its long-range, high-speed reconnaissance run.

Informed sources have stated that fewer than five B-52/D-21 operational sorties were conducted because problems arose over the recovery of at least one of the vital reconnaissance cassettes ejected from the drone. Descending by parachute, the MARS-equipped recovery vehicle failed to capture the unit. In the subsequent water recovery attempt a US Navy destroyer from the alternate recovery force snagged the floating parachute and keel-hauled the reconnaissance package. This programme was also cancelled early due to operational difficulties, political considerations, and the relatively high cost of these limited-duration flights.

On 5 January 1967, 33 year-old Walter L Ray, an Agency pilot, was flying 60-6928 on a routine training sortie from Groom Lake when he suffered a fuel emergency. Forced to eject from the aircraft, a malfunction during the seat separation phase of the sequence caused him to become wedged by the large back parachute pack and the seat head rest. Unable to effect successful separation, he was killed when his seat hit the ground.

Following the deployment of three A-12s and three pilots to Kadena in Okinawa, the first operational mission was flown in August 1967. The major task of this operation was to fly in support of military operations in Southeast Asia. Other areas were also targetted, but remain highly classified. These sorties, flown during a 60-day TDY that each operational pilot 'pulled', on the island, acquired a vast amount of high quality reconnaissance.

On 28 December 1967 Mel Vojvodich, an Agency pilot left Groom Lake's runway in 60-6929, article 126. Having just undergone some major modification work, this Functional Check Flight (FCF), was to ensure that all systems functioned and performance criteria were met. In the shortest flight ever of a 'Blackbird', Vojvodich lost control at about 100 ft (30 m) above the ground and less than seven seconds into the flight. He had to eject. His luck held and he landed safely, despite narrowly missing the fireball of '6929 as it crashed into the ground. During the subsequent investigation it was discovered that the SAS had been wired up incorrectly. The effects of this error on the pilot's control inputs were so severe that Vojvodich had no time to identify the problem and override the system.

The Agency's brief, but highly successful overseas operational liason with the A-12 ended tragically on 5 June 1968. Jack Weeks set out in '6932 from Kadena on what was to be the last A-12 operational flight from the island. He did not return. An inflight problem of unknown nature caused the airplane to crash into the sea roughly 500 miles (926 km) east of Manila in the Philippines and 600 miles (1111 km) south of Okinawa.

Using manned aircraft to monitor strategic targets deep within the confines of a powerful sovereign state had become politically unacceptable. Satellite technology had rendered such operations redundant. The US Air Force took on the Parpro task of monitoring peripheral targets and provided a capability to conduct survivable penetration operations in wartime with a 'new' two-seat aircraft—the R-12 or SR-71.

Chapter 2
The YF-12A

During the late 1950s a specification was drawn up to provide a fire control and missile system for the North American F-108 interceptor. This Improved Manned Interceptor (IMI) was to be Mach 3.0 capable and its ASG-18 pulse-Doppler radar system, developed in parallel with the GAR-9 missile by Hughes, would have a look-down/shoot-down capability for head-on attacks. Furthermore the system advanced the maximum range of the airborne intercept monopulse systems then in use from 40 miles to the region of 120 miles.

As development of both aircraft and avionics progresses, a Convair B-58 (serial 5665) was bailed to Hughes to act as a system testbed. Delivered to the Hughes main plant at Culver City California, it was on the ground in excess of a year whilst re-configuring work prepared it for the missile and fire control system (FCS) flight test programme. Whilst this was being undertaken, Hughes engineers were using high speed film techniques and a 9 ft (2.7 m) deep pit, filled with foam to analyse separation and pitch characteristics of the 818 lb (372 kg) missile. Vehicle separation was provided by two thrusters, one located at each end of the missile. On firing these propulsive charges unlocked the missile from its rail then forced the missle down, clear of the aircraft. At a finite time, its rocket motor ignited and the GAR-9 sped away.

On completion of modifications to B-58 '665, the programme was moved to the Hughes facility on Contractors Row at Edwards. Despite the cancellation of the F-108 programme on 23 September 1959, Department of Defense Officials decided that the outstanding FCS and missile development programme should continue on a 'stand alone' basis. A number of flights followed, and the highly instrumented B-58 and ASG-18 was thoroughly checked out during head-on attacks against manned target aircraft. But progress during this first year of flight testing was slow. B-58 accidents throughout SAC caused numerous groundings of '665. During this off-and-on testing time, a question arose concerning the effectiveness of the ASG-18's ability to detect an extremely low-altitude target. It was settled to some degree when the system actually locked onto and tracked a B-57 at long-range as the target did a 'touch-and-go' landing at Edwards.

On 16–17 March 1960 Kelly Johnson discussed with General Hal Estes and Dr Courtland Perkins, the Air Force Secretary for Research and Development, plans to build an interceptor version of the A-12. Johnson's ideas were keenly received and subsequently forwarded to General Martin Demler at Wright Field for further discussion and analysis. Soon after, General Demler directed Johnson to equip an A-12 variant with the Hughes ASG-18 FCS and GAR-9 missile system. It was envisaged that the design would provide an effective defence against the manned bomber threat throughout the entire NORAD area of responsibility, which covered the whole of North America. The two approaches to this vast defence problem were either to deploy a large number of relatively short-range interceptors, or to use a weapon system possessing a high cruise speed and longer range such as the YF-12. In the latter case, fewer interceptors would be needed. Lockheed was contracted to build three test aircraft for this project, which subsequently bore the article numbers of 1001, 1002 and 1003, they were serialled 60-6934, 60-6935 and 60-6936 respectively.

Hughes' chief pilot, James D Eastham had flown every sortie relating to the missile and radar system on the B-58. The company also provided the Fire Control Operators (FCOs), two of whom occupied the tandem positions behind Eastham. Their task was to monitor the entire system and fire the GAR-9. During the course of this programme Tony Byline, Lyn Gear, John Moore, Jess Le Van, John Archer and, later George Parsons and Ray Scalise all became intimately familiar with these duties.

The North American F-108 Rapier interceptor was designed to have a maximum speed of Mach 3, its two General Electric J93-GE-3 turbojets developing 30,000 lb (13,636 kg) of thrust in afterburner. Proposed as an Improved Manned Interceptor (IMI), the F-108 was killed by high development costs and a more realistic assessment of the manned bomber threat (Rockwell International)

The second year of flight testing involved integrating the missile into the aircraft and tailoring it to work with the radar system. This extremely complex task was carried out under the direction of Mr Clare Carlson, the programme manager, and involved some of the finest electrical engineers in the Western world. As the B-58 test programme continued, captive flights were made. This involved making runs against manned target aircraft, checking out both the radar and missile system to the point of launch. Subsequent analysis of this recorded data would isolate problems that were not apparent to the flight crew during the sortie. After missile separation tests, which included some unguided firings, approximately six live guided firings were made by the B-58 over White Sands missile range in New Mexico during 1961.

In early 1962 Jim Eastham was invited into the Oxcart programme. He joined that summer after an extensive security check. Seconded by Hughes to Lockheed, Eastham, a long-standing friend of Lou Schalk, was a highly skilled pilot. He possessed unparalleled knowledge in the field of flight testing missile and radar systems and was therefore the ideal test pilot/engineer to evaluate the YF-12A. The B-58, similar in size to the A-12, helped Eastham to quickly become familiar with the aircraft. He spent a great deal of time with sub-system engineers, talked to Lou Schalk about flying the A-12, and sat in the cockpit to familiarize himself with the location of switches and other specialized equipment. The early model A-12 was powered by J75s, (a powerplant Eastham was thoroughly familiar with because of his background on the F-106 programme). After several taxying trials, Eastham took to the air during the summer of 1962 in A-12 number three, 60-6926. The flight lasted about one hour.

Eastham continued to fly the B-58 regularly at Edwards, while spending the majority of his time up at Groom Lake with the A-12 flight test programme. Lou Schalk and Kelly Johnson agreed that Jim Eastham should be the first pilot to fly the YF-12, and in March 1963 he began writing the flight handbook. This complicated volume consisted of 12 sections, which covered every aspect of normal and emergency operation. This large-scale writing effort involved moving in with each engineering section concerned with the particular sub-system. A good deal of time was also spent with aerodynamicists to discuss the differences between the A-12 and YF-12. Externally,

these were typified by the fuselage 'chines' being cut back to incorporate a radar radome which housed a 40-inch (60-cm) scanning dish. This modification degraded directional stability to such an extent that three ventral fins were required. A large hinged fin was mounted under the fuselage and two short fixed fins attached under each nacelle. Retraction and extension of the ventral fin worked out of phase with the cycling of the landing gear. In short, when the gear was retracted, the fin extended and vice versa.

Following the truckborne arrival of the prototype article 1001, from Burbank to Groom Lake, several weeks were spent assembling the aircraft and equipping it with the new J58 engines. Little in the way of a fire control system was installed at this stage and after a few wrinkles in the electrical system were ironed out, engine runs were made. Hydraulics were checked to ensure they functioned correctly and were leak-free. The SAS was brought on line and checked to ensure it would engage and function properly. Further ground tests on the J58s involved operating at full power to insure that their output agreed with

James D Eastham, the test pilot who flew the YF-12 on its maiden flight, stands in front of the Convair YB-58A Hustler (55-665) which he piloted during the development of the Hughes ASG-18 intercept radar system. The blisters located on either side of the nose are infrared sensors (Hughes Aircraft via Jim Eastham)

Pratt & Whitney's performance data schedule.

Early taxi tests uncovered a slight problem in the brake and damper system. Once these problems were resolved, a high-speed taxi test was undertaken to near takeoff speed, whereupon power was chopped and the brake 'chute was deployed. Having satisfied all the ground requirements and determined that all instrumentation and communication equipment functioned properly, the YF-12 was deemed to be ready for its maiden flight.

On 7 August 1963, Jim Eastham climbed aboard 60-6934 for a first flight which he modestly characterized as a typical production test flight,

'Snoopy 1', YB-58A 55-665 taking off from Edwards AFB in 1964 piloted by Jim Eastham. Obvious differences from the standard B-58 are the re-profiled nose for the ASG-18 radar and the camera pods under the outboard J79 engines to record GAR-9 missile launches (via Jim Eastham)

chased by Lou Schalk flying an F-104. On that smooth flight, the YF-12s powerplants, control system, and SAS were first checked for proper operation and the electrical, hydraulic, environment and pressurization systems were checked as satisfactory. Finally, the vertical instrument indicating Mach number and knots equivalent airspeed (KEAS) functioned well—this kind of instrumentation was vetoed by the bomber-minded generals at SAC for the SR-71 in preference for 'old standard' round dials. Some minor handling quality checks were conducted followed by an appraisal of the aircraft's static stability. Checked in all three flight axis, the

YF-12 appeared, at least subsonically, to be 'much the same as its stable mates'. Because of its stability, Eastham was of the opinion that the aircraft 'carried enough tail'. With all systems functioning well, the power levers were advanced into full military power and the aircraft went supersonic. This venture presented no problems in either the transonic or low supersonic regions, where handling characteristics were again assessed as identical to those of the A-12. After deceleration to subsonic speed, the airplane was prepared for landing back at The Ranch. Upon lowering the gear, a cockpit light indicated that the ventral fin had retracted—visually confirmed by Lou Schalk in the F-104 flying chase. The approach phase was characterized as identical to that of the A-12. Concern over available ground clearance of the ventral fins during flare proved negative and the near-perfect 'squawk free' test flight ended with the successful deployment of the drag 'chute.

Having completed its first flight with flying colours, there was little urgency in getting the YF-12 out to design speed, since the full speed envelope had

The YF-12 prototype 60-6934, article number 1001, side number FX-934, in matt black/natural metal finish. Interestingly, the 'port hole' just aft of the RSO's canopy is merely black paint designed to confuse onlookers. '934 is still operational with the 9th SRW as a two-seat SR-71C (Lockheed-California)

Jim Eastham (left of picture) with FCO Ray Scalise in front of a YF-12A; they each have a portable air conditioning unit for their pressure suits. Jim Eastham's allocated callsign was 'DUTCH 52' (via Jim Eastham)

LEFT
YF-12 '934 at Edwards AFB displaying the Aerospace Defense Command (ADC) emblem on its vertical fins when it participated in joint flight tests with Air Force Systems Command
(Lockheed-California)

TOP
The YF-12 prototype 60-6934 which made its maiden flight on 7 August 1963. To maintain directional stability at high Mach the YF-12 featured a large ventral fin which folded for takeoff and landing to avoid ground clearance problems

YF-12 '934 sports an immaculate paint scheme as it taxies at Edwards
(Lockheed-California)

Gear up! YF-12 '934 makes a fast getaway from Edwards at the start of a test sortie. The ventral fin is in the folded postion position and the aircraft displays the ADC emblem (Lockheed-California)

already been achieved with the A-12 sistership. Time was spent installing the fire control system instead, ensuring it integrated into the YF-12, and testing the inertial navigation system.

During the Saturday morning announcement by President Johnson, concerning the existence of the 'A-11' programme, YF-12s 60-6934 and 60-6935 were flown from Groom Lake to Edwards by Lou Schalk and Bill Park, thereby lending credibility to the President's 'political brag' and diverting attention away from Area 53 and the Agency programme. At Edwards a low key 'buzz' had gone out to a few senior pilots and maintenance staff, to the effect that something special might be happening on the first morning of their weekend off. In consequence, a dozen or so people witnessed the arrival of two beautifully sleek airplanes that had never before been seen by anyone outside the programme—except for desert dwellers and the occasional incredulous sighting by airline crews. Lou Schalk remembers taxying to the assigned hangar as eyes bulged and heads nodded in utter disbelief. 'Our rather low-key, laid back re-positioning flight lost a touch of elegance when, to aid push-back into the hangar, we turned the aircraft through 180° at the entrance. This turnround sent hot engine exhaust gases flooding into the hangar which caused the overhead fire extinguisher valves to open. These valves were big—like the flood valves on the hangar decks of aircraft carriers—and the desert hadn't seen so much water since Noah's embarkation!'

The third YF-12, 60-6936, soon joined the other two at Edwards and the now overt programme continued in a totally new environment. Suddenly, it appeared the US Air Force had virtually matched, man-for-man, all the contractors involved on the programme and it began to look to the civilian test force that the Air Force was trying to take over the entire project. The move also caused logistical headaches as most of the expertise was to be found back at Area 53. Several people intimately involved in this project have said that the YF-12 was considered the stepchild of the 'Blackbird' family, and received neither the emphasis or the backing from Lockheed

YF-12 '934 with the ventral fin extended; the camera pods under the engine nacalles recorded the launch characteristics of the XAIM-47A missiles (Lockheed-California)

management enjoyed by the two reconnaissance variants. Notwithstanding these 'ripples on the mill pond', the first order of business shortly after arriving at Edwards was to install and make operational the new electrically controlled air inlet system. Once installed, it took Eastham only three months to complete the envelope extension programme.

Jim Eastham flew all of these flights in the Lockheed operated prototype, 60-6934. A minor problem occurred as the airplane approached its design speed of Mach 3.2, which resulted in a directional oscillation. This discrepancy was noticed immediately and acceleration terminated. On return to Edwards, the cause was found to be instability in the inlet controls—as the aircraft yawed in one direction both spikes reacted to the change as a function of the Beta angle. With the problem identified Eastham attained design speed during the next flight.

Lockheed test pilot Bill Weaver found himself in the unenviable position of flying a YF-12 with ventral fin that stubbornly refused to retract. Demonstrating great piloting skill and determination he successfully landed the aircraft and saved an extremely valuable piece of hardware—but the fin's profile was considerably modified.

With much of the 'pick and shovel work' completed in the B-58, the ASG-18 and GAR-9 missile—the latter redesignated AIM-47—was quickly integrated into the YF-12, where the system transcended its predicted performance figures. The enormous amount of electrical power required to drive the radar was provided by two 60 Kva alternators which embodied their own individual liquid cooling systems. The FCS was located in one of four fuselage chine bays and three AIM-47s would have been carried internally in operational service. Highly instrumented for test purposes, however, the three YF-12s never carried a full missile load aloft.

During the first missile separation test, onboard cameras showed the missile incorrectly aligned. Had the rocket motor ignited, the missile would probably have ended up in the front cockpit. Adjustments were made and the remainder of the test programme proceeded extremely well. In all, approximately 12 live missile firings were made from the YF-12, eight of which were made by Jim Eastham. The remainder were fired by US Air Force crews. An indication of the system's operational potential can be gauged from a test flight flown from Eglin AFB. With the YF-12 maintaining Mach 3.2 while cruising in excess of 80,000 ft (24,390 m), the ASG-18 radar acquired a Boeing JQB-47 drone flying at 1,500 ft (457 m) over the sea. Positioned for a head-on attack, the YF-12 destroyed the target with a single missile from 120 miles. Not surprisingly, the Air Force was extremely impressed. It was calculated that Aerospace Defense Command (ADC) would require 93 F-12 interceptors to replace its ageing F-102 and F-106 interceptor fleet. With a force this size, ADC officials

YF-12 60-6936, complete with three mission stencils under the cockpit to denote successful launches of the XAIM-47A missile (on transport dolly) (Lockheed-California)

were confident that they could provide protection to the entire United States against incoming high-speed, low-level bombers. At that point a long and bitter fight over the appropriation of defence funds began between Secretary of Defense Robert McNamara and the Air Force. But the YF-12 underlined its case by publicly demonstrating its speed and altitude capabilities by setting a series of official records. In April 1965 Jim Eastham flew a number of profile proving sorties that would later allow Air Force crews to fly into the record books. Five years to the day that Francis Gary Powers was shot down by a Soviet SA-2 missile, Col Robert L 'Fox' Stephens flew YF-12 60-6936 to a new absolute altitude record of 80,257 ft (24,390 m). Col Walter Daniel took the absolute speed record over a 500 km closed course and also obtained the 1000 km closed course record.

In April 1964, as the war of words between the Air Force and political masters began to heat up, the head of ADC, General Herbert B Thatcher, said that he would like to have a large IMI fleet operational by 1967. He had not failed to notice that the Department of Defense had decided not to proceed with such a programme, despite giving the impression that such a development was underway via the YF-12. In truth McNamara preferred the F-106X proposal after a national intelligence estimate showed it to be the most cost-effective answer to the predicted Soviet bomber threat. As a result, on three occasions over three years, he took the unprecedented step of denying the Air Force access to $90 million worth of funds which had been appropriated by Congress to begin F-12B production. Questioned during a joint hearing of the Senate Armed Services Committee and Appropriation Defense Sub-Committee McNamara said, 'I feel quite confident that it is not necessary to appropriate money that can't be justified for the weapon system itself, simply to keep the production line open'. Such continued delaying tactics undoubtedly protected funds earmarked for the B-70 bomber and the F-106X (the latter metamorphosized into the F-15 Eagle). Following hearings of the Senate Armed Services Committee

into the future of continental air defence it was decided, in the light of intelligence currently available, to downgrade ADC and render the F-12B 'unnecessary'. The *coup de grace* for the F-12 came when Lockheed were ordered to scrap all related tooling—which was duly broken up and sold at $7\frac{1}{2}$ cents per pound.

After the test programme was completed all three YF-12s were placed in storage at Edwards. But this was not quite the end of the story. The loss of an SR-71B on 11 January 1968 prompted an interesting piece of aviation surgery. After ablation of the

Boeing JQB-47E-45-BO, serial 53-4256, was one of a number of B-47 drones used by Air Force Systems Command during the YF-12/XAIM-47A evaluation programme. Highly instrumented, these aircraft recorded radar performance and missile miss-distance data, and were operated by the 3214 Drone Maintenance Squadron from Eglin AFB, Florida. This aircraft was placed in storage at Davis-Monthan on 20 August 1968 (Norman Taylor)

LEFT
Another view of YF-12 60-6936, side-number FX-936, as it flies over the inhospitable terrain of Death Valley in California; Jim Eastham is the pilot (Lockheed-California)

A menacing study of a YF-12 with its forward-left missile bay door open and infrared sensors clearly visible on the front of the chines. Lockheed's corporate JetStar is parked on the right, one of two prototypes powered by Bristol Siddeley Orpheus turbojets (Lockheed-California)

YF-12 '936 climbing to altitude
(Lockheed-California)

fuselage forebody, the rear of article 1001 was grafted
to the front fuselage of a static test specimen to create
'The Bastard', 64-17981. This so-called SR-71C
replacement trainer first flew on 14 March 1969.
Three test flights were made in just two days and the
aircraft was delivered to Beale. It still flies today
whenever the standard B model conversion trainer is
down for extensive maintenance.

NASA

In 1967 the Ames Research Center of the National
Aeronautics and Space Administration (NASA)
negotiated with the US Air Force for access to early
A-12 wind tunnel data. These tests had been
conducted at Ames sometime earlier in conditions of
utmost secrecy. The Air Force decided to release the
information and in return NASA provided a small
team of highly skilled engineers to work on the SR-71
flight test programme. In the summer of 1967 a team
from the Flight Research Center (FRC) under the
leadership of Gene Matranga was engaged on various
stability and control aspects of the SR-71 flight
research effort at Edwards. This work helped to
speed the SR-71 into the inventory and led to a close

YF-12 '936 as used by Col Robert L 'Fox' Stephens and FCO Lt Col Daniel Andre to set a world speed record over a straight course of 2070.101 mph (3332.862 km/h) on 1 May 1965. A large white cross was painted on the underside to assist tracking cameras on the ground (Lockheed-California)

working relationship between the Air Force and the Blackbird team.

The Office of Advanced Research Technology viewed the F-12 not only as a superb technical achievement but also as a potential source of flight data applicable to future commercial supersonic transports (SSTs). NASA therefore requested an instrumented SR-71 to conduct research, or have their instrumentation packages installed on other USAF/Lockheed research and development aircraft. Unable to accommodate either request, the Air Force offered NASA the two remaining YF-12s in storage at Edwards. With funds available from the cancelled X-15 and XB-70 programmes, NASA accepted the offer and agreed to pay for the operational expenses. ADC supplied maintenance and logistic support and on 5 June 1969 a memorandum of understanding (MoU) was signed between the two parties and announced on 18 July.

Utilization of these high-speed research platforms would be high, since NASA engineers at Langley were interested in using them for aerodynamic experiments and testing advanced structures. In addition, Lewis Research Establishment wanted to study propulsion, while Ames wanted to concentrate on inlet aerodynamics and the correlation of wind-tunnel and flight data. Finally, the aircraft could be used to support various specialized experimentation packages. Taken together it was hoped that many problems 'worked around' during earlier test programmes could be designed out of any future commercial venture to avoid expensive mistakes.

Three months work was needed to ready the two YF-12s (60-6935 and 60-6936) for flight. During this time instrumentation readily available to study aerodynamic loads and structural effects was installed by FRC technicians aboard 60-6935. Strain gauges were installed within the wing and fuselage and thermocouples mounted on the left side of the aircraft to measure high-Mach temperature readings.

TOP LEFT
Brake 'chute doors open, '936 is cosseted by ground crews after returning from its record-braking flight (Lockheed-California)

BOTTOM LEFT
The men who set new speed and altitude records in YF-12 60-6936 on 1 May 1965 (left to right): Col Jim Coonie, Col Walt Daniel, Col Robert L 'Fox' Stephens, Maj Daniel Andre, and Maj Noel Warner (Lockheed-California)

YF-12C 60-6937 was first flown on 3 March 1965 as SR-71A article number 2002, serial 64-17951, and initially used for structures, autopilot, and performance testing by Lockheed. NASA acquired the aircraft from the Air Force in 1971 (NASA)

On 11 December 1969 the joint NASA/US Air Force flight test programme was launched when for the first time in three years a YF-12 climbed away from Edwards. In the front seat was Col Joseph Rogers and Maj Heidelbaugh occupied the FCO position. Phase one of the programme was controlled by the Air Force and consisted of developing procedures establishing limitations for command and control and for working out possible bomber penetration tactics against an interceptor with the YF-12s capabilities. This phase of the programme was terminated rather early during the closing stages of the 63rd flight. 60-6936 had been used throughout the tests by the Air Force but was lost on 24 June 1971. Lt Col Ronald J Layton and systems operator Maj William A Curtis were approaching the traffic pattern before recovery at Edwards when a fire broke out as a result of a fuel line fatigue failure. The flames quickly enveloped the entire aircraft and on the base leg both crew members ejected. '6936 crashed into the middle of the dry lakebed and was totally destroyed.

In contrast the NASA programme was a long-running success. Whilst the YF-12s were being prepared to fly again Donald L Mallick and Fitzhugh L Fulton Jr, the two NASA pilots that flew a majority of the phase two programme, were quickly checked out in the type. Fitz Fulton flew his first mission in the front seat of an SR-71B with Lt Col William Campbell as the instructor pilot. Fulton flew his first YF-12A, '6936, the next day on 5 March followed by further familiarization sorties on 9/11 March.

On 26 March Lt Col 'Bill' Campbell flew Victor Horton in '6935, which marked the first flight of a NASA engineer in the YF-12. Ray Young flew in the back seat a few days later and together these two engineers flew most of the NASA back seat sorties.

YF-12 60-6935 became a real workhorse for NASA. A 'flight loads' research programme pursued by FRC and Langley engineers studied the data. In flight measurements were corrolated against the effects of thermal heating and stress, which together change the aircraft's shape and load distribution pattern. A Hasselblad camera was installed within the fuselage to photograph the structure during moderate G manoeuvers. It revealed that under certain conditions the aft end of the fuselage deflected some 15 cm from the centreline.

A major objective of the flight test programme was to compare actual flight data against that predicted by computers in an effort to assess the accuracy of predictive techniques. In order to predict loads and structural response, NASA had developed two computer modelling programmes using a technique known as finite element analysis. Both Flexstab and Nastran programmes were applied to the YF-12.

After the 22nd flight of '6935 on 16 June 1970, the airplane was grounded for nine months for instrumentation changes. Once these were completed Don Mallick and Victor Horton flew a check flight on 22 March 1971; the folding ventral fin was then removed for four flights to assess directional stability up to Mach 2.8.

The folding ventral fin was re-fitted to YF-12 60-6935 for 'Coldwall' heat-transfer experiments using a centreline pod. On 21 July 1977 ceramic debris from the outer shell were ingested down one engine, resulting in a compressor stall and flameout. Meanwhile, Don Mallick flying chase with Ray Young in 60-6937, experienced a series of 'unstarts'; both aircraft limped back to Edwards for an extended inspection (NASA)

NASA needed more aircraft, and the Air Force supplied an SR-71A (article 2002, serial 64-17951) on 16 July 1971. This aircraft had been involved in the contractor flight test programme from the beginning, but the Air Force stipulated that it should only be used for propulsion testing. The first NASA flight was undertaken by Fitz Fulton and Victor Horton on 24 May 1972.

Studies carried out on various aspects of the aircraft's handling qualities revealed that inlet spike movement and bypass door operations were almost as effective as elevons and rudders in influencing the aircraft's flight path at high speed. Propulsion system and flight control integration was an aspect of control testing tackled by the NASA programme in an effort to improve future mixed-compression inlet design. Airflow disturbance often culminated in an unstart and the accompanying aerodynamic hiccups could hardly be tolerated in a supersonic passenger aircraft. This work led Lewis Research Center to develop a throat-bypass stability system, which was successfully tested on the YF-12. It used relief-type poppet valves in the inlet which could react to internal airflow transients much faster than the bypass doors. This valve-stabilized airflow mechanism complemented the inlet control system by providing sufficient time for the inlet shockwave geometry to reconfigure itself to maintain a 'started' inlet.

Another Lockheed system funded, installed, and tested by NASA technicians and prepared by a Honeywell engineer, proved to successful that it was later fitted to operational SR-71s—the central airborne performance analyser (CAPA). This integrated, automatic support system isolated faults and recorded the performance of 170 subsystems (relating primarily to the inlet controls) on 0.5 inch magnetic tape. Pre-and-post flight analysis of this onboard monitoring and diagnostic system proved highly cost effective and reduced maintenance manhours significantly.

Between 1974 and 1976 a research programme was undertaken by NASA's Langley Research Center to investigate and evaluate titanium and composite materials. This metalurgic database would be useful to support decisions affecting future civil and military supersonic cruise aircraft. Lockheed's Advanced Development Projects (Skunk Works) was the prime contractor for three wing panel samples evaluated. These lightweight structures consisted of a weldbrazed titanium skin-stringer panel, a Rohr-

*The NASA flight test team standing in front of YF-12
60-6935 are (left to right): Ray Young, Fitzhugh
Fulton, Donald Mallick, and Victor Horton
(NASA)*

bond titanium honeycomb-core panel and a
boron/aluminium-titanium core panel. All three
components exceeded strength requirements.

For maximum range at high Mach Number and
high altitude, both flight path and speed parameters
must be precisely controlled. During extended
periods in autopilot, NASA identified deficiencies in
the original system and introduced a two-phase
improvement programme. Short-falls in both the
altitude hold and Mach-hold modes were attributed
to decreased aircraft stability, low static pressure, and
temperature variations.

The altitude-hold mode received data via the air
data computer through the pitot static system. Low
atmospheric static pressure made precise control
difficult because of poor instrument resolution.
During the first phase of the improvement programme, the altitude hold-mode was improved by
compensating for angle of attack static pressure
sensitivity and pitot static tube bending.

Cruising on Mach-hold at Mach 3.2 and above
80,000 ft (24,390 m), the aircraft would often be
subjected to altitude variations of as much as $\pm$ 3,000
ft (914 m). This unacceptable situation was caused by
a combination of high-altitude and high-speed which
sometimes leads to an inbalance between kinetic and
potential energy; in turn, large altitude changes are
often necessary to correct for small Mach-Number
changes. The second major objective of the autopilot
improvement programme was to develop an autothrottle control system which could control Mach or
KEAS. The programme was so successful that the
Air Force incorporated the modifications to both
modes.

One of the more unusual heat-transfer experiments supported by NASA was 'Coldwall'. All of
these tests were flown by Fitz Fulton with Vic Horton
as test engineer. For these test flights a hollow,

Fitzhugh Fulton and Ray Young in YF-12 60-6935 in loose formation with NASA Northrop T-38 Talon chase aircraft N923NA
(NASA)

OVERLEAF
A rare shot of the SR-71 (in YF-12C guise, nearest the camera) and a YF-12 in formation with another Johnson design, an F-104 Starfighter flown by John Manke
(NASA)

YF-12 60-6935 during the final seconds of its last ever flight before touching down at Wright-Patterson AFB to become a museum exhibit (Lockheed-California)

stainless steel cylinder was mounted under the fuselage of YF-12 '6935 equipped with thermo-couples and pressure-sensing equipment. It was then encased in a ceramic shell closed off at each end. Before flight, the cylinder was filled with liquid nitrogen to supercool it down to about minus 60°F. At Mach 3.0 the ceramic shell was ballistically removed, resulting in a classic heat transfer experiment as the cylinder went from very cold to very hot almost instantaneously. Using the same cylinder, this experiment was then repeated in a wind tunnel, thereby validating ground research methods for future heat transfer experiments. It was a relatively difficult test to fly, since it was important to be at the proper speed and altitude over the test range and to minimize the flight time at high-speed and high temperature. On 21 October 1976, instruments fired the ceramic coating off prematurely when the sensors got too hot. These sorties were also interesting since Don Mallick had the added difficulty of flying close formation in '6937 in a Mach 3 chase aircraft.

Aircraft 60-6937 was retired from the programme after its 88th flight with NASA on 28 September 1978. It is in storage at Palmdale and still available for future test flights. YF-12 number 60-6935 continued operating until the flight programme ceased after its 145th NASA flight, flown by Fitz Fulton and Victor Horton on 31 October 1979. A week later, Col J Sullivan and Col R Uppstrom ferried the aircraft to the Air Force museum at Wright-Patterson AFB, Ohio, where the sole example of the YF-12 is on permanent display.

Chapter 3
Blackworld Blackbird

In early January 1961 Kelly Johnson set out a new proposal to Dr Joseph Charyk, Secretary of the Air Force, Col Leo Geary, the YF-12 project officer at the Pentagon, and Lew Meyer, a financial officer in the Air Force, for a strategic reconnaissance bomber designated the R-12. It was originally envisaged that the airplane's role could be interchangeable, thus enabling it to carry out the dual tasks of bombing and reconnaissance.

An external pod (similar to that used on the B-58) to carry the bombload was proposed, but rejected on weight, cost, and utility grounds. Instead cameras and stores were to be carried internally in the fuselage chine bays; this would minimize the effects of drag, and preserve the airplane's small radar cross section (RCS).

Encouraged to continue their company funded studies, an Air Force evaluation team reviewed the design and mockup on 4 June 1962 and were suitably impressed. As discussions continued with the Department of Defense and General Curtis Le May (commander of SAC), substantial opposition was encountered from some senior Air Force officers, who saw the proposals as a direct threat to 'their' ailing B-70 programme. When McNamara and his advisors decided that there was no requirement for a Mach 3 + weapons delivery platform, the reconnaissance strike (RS) designation was retained for political reasons, despite the fact that the airplane would later be used purely for reconnaissance purposes.

An 'error' made by President Johnson during his second announcement concerning the programme led Lockheed to change the airplane's designation to be consistent with his speech. The transposition of two letters from RS to SR enables a more accurate descriptive designation to be applied to the airplane—strategic reconnaissance.

On 27–28 December 1962 Lockheed were placed on contract to build six production test aircraft.

Invaluable experience gained as a member of the A-12 contractor test force had equipped Robert J Gilliland admirably for a premier post. In the summer of 1964 Kelly Johnson offered him the position of project pilot for the Lockheed SR-71. Accepting immediately, Bob Gilliland continued flying other Lockheed experimental programmes while attending meetings and following the development of article number one, 2001. The prototype SR-71A, serial 64-17950 was delivered to Site II, Air Force Plant 42, Building 210, at Palmdale on 29 October 1964. In early December Kelly and Gilliland flew from Burbank to Palmdale in the twin-engined prototype Jetstar to review final assembly progress. On arrival Bob Murphy, Lockheed's chief production engineer at Palmdale, showed the two men around building 210. Bob Gilliland was dismayed to see article number one spread all over the hangar floor. On return to Burbank and mindful that a lot of brass from Omaha, Wright-Pat, and Washington were planning to attend the first flight scheduled for December 22, Gilliland said to Kelly, 'Maybe we better postpone this thing 'til after Christmas. It is liable to be a little embarrassing to you, to me, and to the Skunk Works if we get them out here and we don't go'. Kelly replied, 'Nope. If I postponed things everytime somebody wanted me to postpone, it would still be in the jigs.'

During those final weeks leading up to the first flight Bob Gilliland recalls having to attend frequent meetings, which he often found tedious and 'in great danger of analysis-paralysis'. The principle agenda of discussion was exactly which systems would be operational during the maiden flight. The criterion was supposed to be 'safety of flight'. Anyone that has experience of test flying will know that this rather vague subjective term leaves tremendous latitude for honest differences of opinion. Entering fully into these discussions with all the engineers involved with each item Gilliland knew that he, the guy who would

A classic study of an SR-71 Blackbird as it taxies out for takeoff at Beale AFB (Lockheed-California)

TOP RIGHT
The SR-71 prototype on its way from Burbank to Palmdale on 29 October 1964

RIGHT
Arrival. The SR-71 prototype is safely delivered to Site II at Palmdale for final assembly (Lockheed-California via Bob Murphy)

take the airplane aloft, would be the final arbiter.

The flight test engineering effort was led by Richmond L (Dick) Miller Jr. He prepared the plan for the entire contractor test programme. Once this had been approved, he became responsible for the selection of tests to be accomplished on individual flights. There was some discussion as to whether the first flight should be flown subsonically, with the gear down, or whether the gear should be raised and, if all went well, the aircraft flown supersonically. It was agreed that should there be a serious problem during the flight, no dead-stick landing would be attempted and if upon gear retraction it subsequently failed to extend, the aircraft would not be landed on its belly. Ejection would be preferable in either case. A 'jump out' and consequent loss of a prototype is a fate to be

avoided as it leads to programme costs soaring into megabucks; first, second, and third tier vendors are waiting for validated flight test to proceed with series production and reduce unit costs.

Although the aircraft could be supported on its jack points in the hangar and the 3000 psi hydraulic system artificially activated with the engine off, and systems such as the flight controls and landing gear exercised, the fear was that the system may not work in actual flight since the aircraft is then supported aerodynamically causing the added complication of extreme vehicle aeroelasticity, which could cause minute tolerances and electrical sequencing to malfunction. In the event, Kelly decided to go for broke and attempt to fully exercise the aircraft.

Article number 2001, serial 64-17950, the SR-71 prototype is prepared for its first engine test run on 18 December 1964 (Lockheed-California)

RIGHT
Robert J Gilliland, the first man to fly the SR-71 (Lockheed-California)

As '950 approached completion the manufacturing effort was reinforced by the flight test engineers. Fuel flows, flow rates, and pump sequencing received close attention because the fuel system in the SR-71 is of greater capacity than the other 'Blackbirds'. For the first flight it was decided that only a light fuel load would be carried to improve controllability in the event of an engine failure on takeoff. This would also allow the aircraft to be landed immediately during an inflight emergency, instead of remaining airborne to dump fuel.

In addition to a controllability concern, there was also the potential problem of a partial fuel load causing cavitation of the fuel pumps. On takeoff, fuel flow indicators rev up digitally to incredible totals. Tank number one sits well forward, just aft of the cockpits and has more fuel pumps in it than other tanks because it is used for trimming the CG since it has a greater moment arm. With light fuel loads it is therefore essential that tank sequencing is correct and that the fuel pumps are not starved of fuel by sloshing, frothing, or fuel inadequency. In short, fuel starvation on takeoff leading to a double engine flame-out would be very embarrassing.

Once completed, '950 was placed on jacks and hydraulically operated systems were checked for movement rates, ranges and direction. Frequency response checks were carried out to verify servomechanism functions. Vibration tests for flutter analysis and prediction, electronic flight control augmentation under simulated operating conditions, and a host of other tests were completed, designed to exercise the whole gamut of aircraft systems required. Final checks were made during engine ground runs, the first of which was conducted 18 December 1964. With all systems operating throughout the ranges possible on the ground, a check could be made of the aircraft operating as an independent entity, as in flight.

Fully briefed on all systems operating characteristics flying the engineering flight simulator and the A-12, an aircraft with similar qualities, Bob Gilliland was able to become as thoroughly familiar with expected flight characteristics.

On 21 December 1964 a 'non-flight' operation, written up by Bob Gilliland and Dick Miller was scheduled. All preflight checks were carried out as if the flight were to leave the ground—including

checking oxygen redundancy. Each engine was then fired up alternatively and control movements, all lights, gauges, switches and indicators scrutinized. External checks for hydraulic leaks or other abnormal behaviour were checked and co-ordinated between the pilot and ground crews. With the trim system, centre of gravity ejection system, and all radios checked, Gilliland taxied out, checking nose gear steering, anti-skid and engine operation en route to the runway. On arrival at the hammer head, wheels were chocked and each engine run-up to full military power and trimmed individually with micro fuel adjustment to develop maximum thrust without overtemping. With permission from ATC to taxi 'into position and hold', '950 moved onto runway 25 at Palmdale. Holding on the brakes, Gilliland advanced both engines to military power, checked all engine parameters released the brakes and then simultaneously moved power levers into 'min-burner'. The burners lit a little asymmetrically as Gilliland smoothly increased power to max throttle lever angle. In the meantime engine instruments were racing upwards, taking a while to stabilize. The SR-71 accelerated rapidly—due in part to the light

fuel load. Then at around 120 knots (222 km/h) Bob snapped the throttles to idle—making sure not to pull them to idle cut-off. He then deployed the 40 ft (12 m) drag chute. 'It throws you almost as hard against the shoulder straps as landing on an aircraft carrier'. Shedding the 'chute at 50 knots (92 km/h), he turned off the runway and taxied back in to park. All went relatively well and minor 'squawks' were noted and fixed before the final preparations were completed for the first flight.

The day of the first flight dawned cold and relatively clear. Bob Gilliland proceeded up to Palmdale from his home in Flintridge, Pasadena, across the Angeles Crest mountains (which encircle the Los Angeles basin and rise over a mile high) then over into the Mojave Desert to Palmdale. At the airfield he met Dick Miller and Bob Murphy, discussed the weather and status of the SR-71. Murphy told Gilliland that '950 was 'ready', but there still remained a few 'open items'—squawks or discrepancies. In all these numbered 375, which may be a record. Bob Gilliland hoped the TDI (triple display indicator) which digitally displayed Mach number, altitude in feet, and knots equivalent

First flight. Chief test pilot Bob Gilliland cruising SR-71 64-17950 over runway 25 for the flyby over Palmdale on 22 December 1964. Jim Eastham is flying chase in F-104A, serial 60790 (Lockheed-California via Jim Eastham)

airspeed, or KEAS (as distinguished from KIAS—knots indicated airspeed)—would be OK, but it was not. He would have to use the pitot static system for airspeed and altitude, which is installed as a backup to the TDI-KEAS.

The flight card—a list of tasks to be attempted by the pilot once airborne, which had been complied by Dick Miller—was signed by him and then by Bob Gilliland—signifying the pilot's agreement.

Gilliland went to his locker and got suited up in a low-altitude environment suit. This could be worn safely to a maximum altitude of 50,000 ft (15,244 m). Flight at higher levels called for a full pressure suit or 'moon suit' to sustain life in the event of an ejection or cockpit decompression.

With long turtleneck underwear on for comfort,

Gilliland's regular orange flight suit sported a 'Lockheed' patch on the front of one side and 'Gil' on the other. Pulling on high-top bailout boots with sponge rubber inserts in each sole, he wore a low-altitude white crash helmet decorated with two small red needle-nosed F-104 decals at the top front on each side. The entire ensemble was finished off by a pair of US Navy orange flight gloves.

For this first flight, it had been decided that the back seat would remain empty for safety reasons. With certain controls and switches only in the rear cockpit, it had been necessary to jury-rig a special instrumentation control panel in the front cockpit to operate certain rear cockpit functions—the IFF (SSR) being one.

Three F-104s were provided as chase aircraft. Lockheed test pilot James D Eastham—later to become the second pilot to fly the SR-71—flew one. The other two were provided by the US Air Force and flown by Col Robert L 'Fox' Stephens and Lt Col Walt Daniels—one of them flew a two seater with a photographer in the back seat.

Bob Gilliland and Dick Miller agreed that flying qualities, all available systems operation, and flight

safety checks would be paramount. The aircraft would be exercised through these and the envelope expansion continued into the supersonic speed regime if initial results were acceptable.

Ensconced in the front seat of '950, Bob started the engines (using a new high-pressure air-starting system devised by Bob Murphy) and taxied out. Pre-takeoff checks completed, he was cleared to hold. Jim Eastham, primary chase, was already airborne and circling above. Gilliland was ready and Eastham was in position.

Gilliland released the brakes and hit the burners. Acceleration was brisk! Leaving runway 25 he climbed the aircraft steeply and headed north. When the gear was up and locked power was reduced to military. The climb continued to moderate altitude, where the aircraft was levelled off and a reasonable speed maintained. At takeoff and as speed increased, airspeed and altitude readings were compared and calibrated with Eastham in the F-104 to verify accurate pitot static system operation.

The flight card next called for manoeuverability and handling checks during static and dynamic stability and control tests. These were carried out

SR-71 64-17950 was destroyed at Edwards AFB on 10 January 1967 during anti-skid brake tests; test pilot Art Peterson escaped unhurt (Lockheed-California via Robert F Dorr)

with the SAS axes on and off, individually and then totally. Performance comparisons of predicted values of speed versus thrust and fuel consumption were made. Bob then climbed the aircraft in military up to about 30,000 ft (9146 m), checking cabin pressure, oxygen and temperature control, tracking north over the towns of Mojave and Cantil, and to the west of China Lake Naval Air Station, on up to Owens Valley, between the Sierra Nevada mountains to the west and the White Mountains to the east—all of this geography lies within the Edwards SOA—special operating area. Just north of Bishop and south of Mammoth and Yosemite National Park, Bob completed a 180° turn to the left and rolled out on a southerly track over the cordillera of the Sierra Nevada.

LEFT
Lockheed test pilot Bill Weaver survived a Mach 3-plus breakup accident at an altitude in excess of 80,000 ft (24,390 m) in SR-71A 64-17952 on 25 January 1966. He is wearing the S901J pressure suit manufactured by the David Clark Company (Lockheed-California)

BELOW
The ill-fated SR-71A 64-17952 refuelling from a Boeing KC-135Q tanker during trials in 1965 (Lockheed-California)

BOTTOM
The distinctive profile of the SR-71B conversion trainer which features a raised rear cockpit. Lockheed's corporate twin-engined JetStar and KC-135 tankers in background (Lockheed-California)

With the aircraft performing well, it was time to go supersonic and the southerly track would ensure that few people would be subjected to the SR-71s powerful sonic boom. Just northwest of Bishop and with Eastham in the F-104 in position, Gilliland hit min-burner, examined engine parameters, then slid the power levers up to maximum and accelerated to 400 KIAS in level flight. At Mach 1.2 a red master caution light illuminated. A glance down at the annunciator panel identified the cause as CANOPY UNSAFE. A glance to both right and left verified that all four hooks holding the titanium and glass canopy in place were fully locked—the sensitive micro switches activated because a low pressure area created aerodynamically by the windscreen caused the canopy to rise up slightly against the hooks holding it in place. In a matter of experience and judgement, Gilliland correctly analysed the situation and continued with the flight—if he'd been wrong, and the canopy had detached itself, the second guessers would have come crawling out of the woodwork to denounce his stupidity, probably adding, 'Why do you think we place a big red light in the cockpit just for that purpose?'

In the event the throttles were again advanced to maximum and the climb and acceleration continued while carefully monitoring all instruments. At 50,000 ft (15,244 m) and Mach 1.5 he eased the power off into military and commenced deceleration first with wings level to 350 KIAS, then slowing and descending to allow proper cooling of the engine rotating element and casing.

Back now in the Palmdale area, he was advised by test ops that Johnson had requested a subsonic flyby down the runway. As this was completed Gilliland wheeled around onto downwind, dumped the gear and saw three greens. Turning now onto a wide base leg, he set up a long final flying slightly hot, at about 185 knots (278 km/h). Having rolled the weight on the mains, the nose was gently lowered, drag chute deployed, jettisoned at about 50 knots (92.5 km/h), and the roll out allowed to continue to the end of runway 25. Gilliland turned '950 off the active and taxied to the ramp: 'DUTCH 51' was down.

After congratulations from Johnson and others the last order of business was the debriefing. There were between a dozen and 30 engineers and vendors in attendance. When all were settled down Bob Gilliland turned on a tape recorder, stated his name, date, aircraft serial number, and then proceeded to describe the flight chronologically from startup to shutdown. After this the Lockheed test engineers headed by Dick Miller asked clarifying questions. Then it was the vendors turn. Afterwards the tape was removed, typed into narrative form, copied and circulated to all concerned. This procedure enabled a quick first look to be made of the flight. Later the two cameras positioned in the canopy and viewing the front instrument panel were removed. This together with data from other 'automatic observer' (AO)

panels enabled the Data Reduction Group, headed by Bob Klinger and later Andy McNicoll, to 'reconstruct' the flight for engineering analysis. So ended that historic maiden flight of 22 December 1964.

Following the first three flights, Dick Miller flew as flight test engineer on virtually all development flights except those for limit structural tests which are always flown with the pilot only. '951 and '952 were added for contractor development of payload systems and techniques, shortly after the development aircraft test programme started and additional Lockheed test pilots were brought into the programme. These included Jim Eastham, Bill Weaver, and Art Peterson.

The concentrated efforts of Lockheed were matched by those at Air Force Systems Command (AFSC) Headquarters, Wright-Patterson AFB, Ohio. Here, Col Ben Bellis had been appointed the System Project Officer or 'SPO' for the SR-71. His task was to structure a development and evaluation programme that would sound out the newcomer for the Air Force. Implementation of this programme would be undertaken by the SR-71/YF-12 Test Force at the Air Force Flight Test Center at Edwards. Here AFSC test pilots would work in parallel with their Lockheed counterparts for contractor development. Both Phase I experimental and Phase II developmental test flying had moved to Edwards, where '953, '954 and '955 were evaluated by 'blue suiters'.

1965 saw the SR-71 undertaking air refuelling tests, which soon became routine. Envelope expansion proceeded well as did a host of other tests. On 2 November Bob Gilliland and Bill Weaver completed the maiden flight of the first of two SR-71B pilot trainers. By the close of that year Kelly Johnson could be justifiably pleased with the progress of his new 'Blackbird'.

The first losses

On 25 January 1966, Bill Weaver and RSO Jim Zwayer took off from Edwards AFB in SR-71A '952. Both were Lockheed employees.

The objectives of the flight were to evaluate the navigation and reconnaissance systems, as well as to investigate procedures for improving high mach cruise performance by reducing trim drag. This required that CG be scheduled further aft than normal to compensate for the rearward shift of C of P at high Mach. After in-flight refueling from a KC-135 tanker, 'DUTCH 64' climbed back to cruising speed and altitude. Shortly thereafter, an inlet scheduling malfunction was experienced. This was followed by an unstart of the right engine while in a 30° banked turn to the right at approximately 80,000 ft (24,390 m) and a speed of over Mach 3.0. The cumulative effect of malfunctions, configuration, speed, altitude and attitude resulted in forces being exerted on the aircraft that exceeded the restoring authority of the flight controls and SAS. This led to a breakup of the aircraft, with the entire forebody becoming detached.

SR-71A 64-17952: the extended UHF antenna below the cockpit is retracted prior to high-speed flight (Lockheed-California)

As soon as it became apparent that the situation was hopeless, Bill tried to tell Jim, over the intercom, what was happening and to try and stay with the aircraft until they were down to a lower speed and altitude, as he didn't think it would be possible to eject successfully under such conditions. Unfortunately, as revealed upon subsequent recovery of the cockpit voice recorder, most of the words of the transmission were completely garbled and unintelligible due to the incredibly high G forces both men were being subjected to at this time. At this point, Bill blacked out and, to this day, doesn't know how he escaped. Indeed, his ejector seat was found still inside the cockpit section amongst the wreckage.

During the breakup of the aircraft, the cockpit canopies were probably blown off and a combination of G forces and air loads caused both men to be blasted out into space. Bill Weaver now takes up the story.

'I thought I was having a bad dream and hoped that I would wake up and all this would go away. However, as I began to regain consciousness, I realized it was not a dream and that this had really happened. At that point, I thought I was dead because I was convinced that I could not have survived what had happened. I remember thinking that being dead wasn't so bad after all. I had kind of a detached, euphoric feeling. As I became more conscious, I realized I wasn't dead after all, and that I somehow became separated from the aircraft. I couldn't see anything as my face visor had iced up.

'My pressure suit had inflated, so I knew the emergency oxygen supply in the seat kit attached to the parachute harness was functioning. This provided not only breathing oxygen and pressurization essential at those altitudes, but also physical protection against the intense buffeting and G forces

75

SR-71A 64-17954 was written off after an aborted takeoff accident on 11 April 1969. Lt Col Bill Skliar and RSO Maj Noel Warner emerged unscathed (US Air Force via Robert F Dorr)

I had been subjected to. It was like being in your own life support capsule. After realizing that I wasn't dead and that I was free of the aircraft, I was concerned about stability and not tumbling at such high altitude. Centrifugal forces sufficient to cause physical damage can be generated if the body tumbles at high altitude where there is little air density to resist these motions. Fortunately, the small stabilization 'chute designed to prevent tumbling had worked just fine.

'My next concern was the main 'chute; would the barometric automatic opening device work at 15,000 ft (4573 m)? I certainly hadn't made a proper exit—I knew I had not initiated the ejection procedure. How long had I been blacked out and how high was I? I was about to open the face plate so that I could see and try to estimate my altitude and locate the parachute 'D' ring, when I felt the sharp, reassurring tug indicating the main 'chute had deployed. This was a very reassuring feeling, believe me. I managed to raise the face plate and the visibility was just incredible. It was a clear, winter day, about three o'clock in the afternoon and from my vantage point beneath the parachute canopy it appeared that I could see for a couple of hundred miles. But what made everything just perfect was that about $\frac{1}{4}$ of a mile away was Jim's 'chute. I was delighted, because I didn't believe either of us could have survived, and to think that Jim had also made it gave me an incredible lift.

'I couldn't manipulate the risers to steer my 'chute because my hands were frozen and I needed one hand to keep my iced up vizor raised (the latch was broken). As a result, I could only see in one direction and the terrain wasn't at all inviting. I was convinced we'd have to spend at least the night out there and I was trying to think of things I had been taught in survival

SR-71A 64-17953 crashed on 18 December 1969 after an inflight explosion. Lt Col Joe Rogers and RSO Lt Col Garry Heidlebaugh ejected safely (Lockheed-California)

training. I landed okay and was trying to undo my parachute harness when I heard a voice say 'Can I help you'. I looked up and there was a guy walking towards me wearing a cowboy hat and behind him was a helicopter. He turned out to be Albert Mitchell, Jr and, as I learned later, owned the huge cattle ranch in North East New Mexico upon which I had landed. He helped me out of the 'chute, told me he had radioed the police, Air Force and nearest hospital and then said, 'I saw your buddy coming down, I'll go and help him'.

'He climbed into his little helicopter and was back a few minutes later with the devastating news that Jim was dead. I asked him to take me over to see Jim and, after verifying that there was nothing that could be done, other than have his ranch foreman watch over the body until authorities arrived, he flew me to Tucumcari hospital about 60 miles (111 km) to the South. I have vivid memories of that flight, as well. I didn't know much about helicopters, but I knew a lot about red lines, and the airspeed needle was at or above the red line all the way to Tucumcari. I thought about the possibility of that little thing shaking itself apart in flight and how ironic it would be to have miraculously survived the previous disaster only to be finished off in the helicopter that had come to my rescue! We made it without mishap and, on reaching the hospital I was able to phone Lockheed Flight Test at Edwards. They knew the aircraft had been lost, after loss of all radio and radar contact, and just didn't believe that I had survived.'

During the closing stages of 1966 the SR-71 underwent a series of anti-skid brake trials. Bill Weaver conducted most of these and on 10 January 1967 he was due to evaluate the system with the

This specially posed publicity shot gave the TR-1 tactical reconnaissance aircraft a rare opportunity to formate on an SR-71 (Lockheed-California)

aircraft at maximum gross weight. By a twist of fate, he was unable to conduct this particular test because of the funeral of his friend Walt Ray, killed a few days earlier in an A-12 accident. Art Peterson, another Lockheed pilot, was substituted and the RSO position remained empty. Entering a flooded test area of the Edwards runway at well over 200 knots (370 km/h), the brake 'chute failed to deploy properly. Wheel brakes remained ineffective until the airplane had cleared the test area. Once on a dry surface the brakes locked the wheels and all six main tyres blew. As momemtum carried the aircraft on, the brakes burned out. Magnesium wheel hubs were consumed on the concrete runway and triggered a fire. Now riding on the main gear stumps, Peterson skillfully managed to retain control of the stricken aircraft until he ran out of runway. On the overrun, one of the main gear legs dug into the dry lake bed, causing side forces to rip the nosewheel leg off. This simultaneously stopped the aircraft and broke its back. Fire now quickly spread to engulf the entire aircraft, but Peterson managed to extract himself from the cockpit—despite sustaining back injuries which would ground him for several weeks. For the SR-71 prototype, article, 2001, it was the end of the line. She was written off.

In mid-1966 Bill Skliar left the A-12 programme and became Chief of Operations for the SR-71 test force at Edwards. On 11 April 1969, Lt Col Skliar and his RSO Maj Noel Warner lined up SR-71A, 64-17954, on runway 04 at Edwards and began a maximum gross weight take-off. 'DUTCH 69' had just rotated when one of the left main gear tyres blew. Unable to support the additional weight load the two remaining tyres on that leg also blew. Immediately aborting takeoff, the burning shrapnel from the disintegrating magnesium wheel hubs caused a fire which rapidly took hold of the entire aircraft. Skliar managed to retain control of the aircraft and brought it to a halt on the runway. With the worst of the fire along the left side and a slight breeze from the 5 o'clock position, Skliar exited from the right and then assisted Warner to clear the cockpit, as fire billowed all around them. This courageous pilot continued a distinguished service career; but not so 64-17954, she never flew again. After this incident all SR-71s had their wheels replaced with less combustible aluminium units and B F Goodrich beefed up the tyre compound.

Functioning as an autonomous self-contained unit complete with its own maintenance and support

Lockheed's long-serving SR-71 testbed 64-17955 with 'Skunk Works' badge on fin (Lockheed-California)

facilities, the SR-71/YF-12 Test Force—later redesignated the 4786 Test Squadron on 16 January 1970—reported to General Slay, Commander of the Air Force Flight Test Centre, Edwards AFB.

On 18 December 1969 the units director, Lt Col Joe Rogers and his RSO, Lt Col Gary Heidelbaugh were scheduled to fly 64-17953 on a test sortie. Having been 'off-line' while extensive modifications were undertaken to install a new ECM system, the flight would be '953's first for many weeks. After completing post takeoff tanking from a KC-135, Rogers, an experienced test pilot with more than 200 hours logged on the SR-71, initiated a pre-planned acceleration and climb. Soon after transitioning to supersonic flight, the crew of 'DUTCH 68' heard a loud explosion. This was accompanied by a loss of power and severe control difficulties. As the aircraft decelerated its angle of attack continued to increase, despite pushing the control stick 'hard against the firewall'. Now subsonic and heavy with fuel, both crew members realised that '953 had entered an irrecoverable corner of the flight envelope. Eleven seconds after the explosion Rogers knew it was time to get out—'Let's go'. Both men then safely ejected while the aircraft continued in a deep stall, making its grave near Shoshone, at the southern end of Death Valley, Cal. The precise cause of the explosion remains unknown.

With Phase I and II of the test programme satisfactorily completed, the 4786 Test Squadron at Edwards was deactivated on 12 May 1972. For their pioneering contributions to the A-12, YF-12 and SR-71 projects, Lou Schalk, Bill Park, Jim Eastham and Bob Gilliland received the Iven C Kincheloe Award for 1964, from the Society of Experimental Test Pilots.

Air Force Logistics Command involvement

The Palmdale facility was used as an acceptance test centre. Here, an Advanced Systems Project Officer (ASPO) was established and each new aircraft was subjected to an extensive Functional Check Flight (FCF). Having verified aircraft performance-criteria, each pristine SR-71 would then be delivered to Beale by a 9th SRW crew.

On 31 December 1970 the functions of this unit were transferred to Air Force Logistics Command (AFLC) and Det 51 was created. Established as a sub-division or operating location the unit reported to the Sacramento Air Logistics Center (located at

'Black Bunny', F-4J-29-MC, bureau number 153783, from VX-4 at Point Mugu in California, formates on 'the contractor's bird'—SR-71A 64-17955—in July 1972. This particular F-4J now serves with No 74 Sqn RAF as ZE352
(US Navy via Robert F Dorr)

Norton AFB California), and provided SR-71 maintenance support. This also entailed flying FCFs on completion of scheduled maintenance overhauls and testing and evaluating new upgraded systems. During an FCF from Palmdale on 15 October 1973, Maj Thomas S Pugh and his RSO, Maj Ronald L Selberg experienced a left engine surge just beyond takeoff abort. With little alternative, takeoff was continued despite marginal control. During gear retraction a fire warning light illuminated, swiftly followed by the disintegration of the left engine turbine section. Having managed to accelerate the aircraft to a safe single engine speed, Maj Pugh completed engine shutdown procedures on the left engine, and extinguished an intense fire which had developed as a result of shrapnel damage to hydraulics, fuel, and oil lines. Despite extensive fire damage to the left nacelle, fuselage, and right rudder, an elongated visual traffic pattern was flown, fuel dumped and a safe recovery back to Palmdale executed. Maj Pugh's timely, well co-ordinated actions unquestionably saved the aircraft and he was awarded an Air Force 'well done'.

A reorganization on 1 September 1977 saw the duties of Det 51 at Plant 42 taken over by Det 6. Command of this detachment is also located at Norton, which in turn reports to its parent unit, the 2762 Logistics Squadron based at Wright Patterson AFB, Ohio. Some of the noteworthy evaluations carried out by this unit include; increasing bank angles, digital navigation readouts, improved cockpit lighting, a comprehensive defence systems update, the digital automatic flight inlet control system and synthetic aperture radar. To carry out these and other tests, Det 6 has a dedicated platform, aircraft number six, '955.

During September and October of 1980, '955 equipped with a S-band Space Transportation

*SR-71A 64-17960 is still operational with the 9th SRW.
The Bertia Company developed the high-temperature
hydraulic actuators to power the all-moving fins
(Lockheed-California)*

*Majs K 'Pete' Collins (left) and RSO Conrad Seagroves
after a flight in SR-71A 64-17960. In the
background, ground crews place fans adjacent to the left
main gear to cool the brakes
(Paul F Crickmore Collection)*

SR-71s regularly encounter US Navy F-14 Tomcats from NAS Miramar, located off the coast of San Diego, California. Flying rather higher than SR-71 64-17955, an F-14 from VF-124 holds station during a 'Tom-too-hot' training sortie in 1974 (Grumman History Center)

System ('Shuttle') transponder flew a series of five target missions to evaluate the battery of C-band tracking, communication, and navigation systems that would be trained upon the Orbiter as it re-entered the Earth's atmosphere for landing at Edwards. The high-speed, high-altitude performance of the SR-71 made it an obvious choice for these trials. The first two tests involved C-band radar acquisition of the aircraft. The three S-band tests called for two approaches to Edwards, while the third involved a single approach to the Northrop strip at White Sands Missile Range, New Mexico—a backup STS landing site.

Today, Det 6 has the unique distinction of being the sole unit outside the 9th SRW to fly SR-71s. Their high level of engineering expertize, and systems updates could, if necessary, ensure that The Lady remains a viable reconnaissance platform for many years.

Chapter 4
Technical

The wing is arranged in box sections, one outboard of the engine nacelle and two inboard. The inboard sections are positioned one forward and one aft and separated by a metre wide compartment housing the main gear bay. The front and rear beams of the inboard box sections provide support for the main gear.

Five degrees of conical camber is applied to the outboard wing leading edge to reduce bending movement and torsion in this section, and apply most of its aerodynamic load to the rear of the nacelle. The nacelle, considered an integral part of the wing, acts as a chordwise beam and torque tube for transmitting these loads forward and redistributing them, via the nacelle rings, to the forward and aft box sections. The thin, biconvex wing has a leading edge sweep of 52.62°, a trailing edge sweep forward of 10° and joins the mid-fuselage with a slight negative incidence.

The fuselage can be described in three sections. First the forebody. As the nose section is interchangeable for mission flexibility and structurally independent of the fuselage, the forebody can be said to extend from the tip of the forward cockpit to a point perpendicular to the leading edge of the wing. It consists of a ring stiffened cylinder, fitted with longerons at the top, bottom and side, and modified to include the cockpit, equipment compartments, nose gear well, air refuelling receptacle and two fuel tanks.

The mid-section, which extends to the main undercarriage well, contains fuel tanks stretching laterally into the forward wing box area. The main gear bay dissects the forward and aft wing boxes and forms two structurally independent elements. Inboard, aerodynamic, and bending loads at the root are carried by the fuselage longerons located at the top and bottom of the centreline; outboard, loads are borne by the nacelle and wing attaching structure.

The aft section begins rear of the main gear bay and tapers into the tail, but excludes the brake 'chute recepticle. The entire area, together with the aft wing

section, is used to provide two more large fuel compartments. The longer tail of the SR-71 serves to increase internal fuel capacity and improve fineness ratio. To reduce trim drag at high Mach numbers the nose cants upwards from the centreline some two degrees. Fuselage structural rigidity is enhanced by ring stiffeners while fairings fitted between the fuselage and wing root, although not part of the structure and supporting local airloads only, provide a convenient cavity to house electrical and plumbing lines.

An inherent aerodynamic design characteristic of delta winged aircraft, resulting from their large root chord, is a major rearward shift of the centre of pressure during acceleration from subsonic flight. This results in the pilot having to apply an increasing amount of drag inducing elevon to trim the airplane and reduce the pitch moment. A key aerodynamic asset in reducing trim drag in the SR-71 is its chine. With the fuselage forebody accounting for 40 per cent of the aircraft's overall length, the chine acts as a fixed canard surface, producing lift as a function of the square of the speed, becoming more effective as Mach number increases. This, combined with the long moment arm of the forebody in relation to the centre of gravity, greatly reduces the rearward translation of

TOP LEFT
The YF-12A (left) and SR-71A in the pre-contact position before refuelling. In addition to its full chine, the SR-71 also has an extended boat-tail at the end of the rear fuselage
(Lockheed-California)

BOTTOM LEFT
The unusual main gear configuration of the SR-71 is well illustrated on this landing shot. Thanks to the hollow axle design of the undercarriage leg, any wheel can be changed without removing the other two
(Sgt G L Jones)

the centre of pressure and in turn reduces the amount of elevon to balance these forces, reducing trim drag. The chine also offers benefits when manoeuvering at low speed. As incidence increases, there is an increase in suction over the upper surface, particularly at the leading edge wing tip. This creates an adverse pressure gradient behind the leading edge which separates, rolls into a vortex, turns downstream and shed at the wing tip. As incidence is increased further, the separated flow moves inboard until the complete leading edge inherits a continuous vortex. This allows both a lower approach speed and the use of smaller vertical surfaces to retain minimum longitudinal stability, while additionally reducing rolling moment due to yaw at high angles of attack.

The maximum trimmed lift/drag ratio is 6.5 at Mach 3.0 and approximately 11.5 at subsonic flight. Directional stability benefits inherent in the chine can be clearly demonstrated by direct comparison between the SR-71 and YF-12. In order to accommodate the Hughes AN/ASG-18 fire-control radar, the chine was cut back to the front cockpit. The loss of directional stability required more tail. This was provided by drag inducing, twin ventral fins on the underside of the nacelles, and a large folding centreline ventral fin.

As well as their aerodynamic benefits, the chines provide the main accommodation for internally

The surface temperatures generated on the SR-71 in the cruise

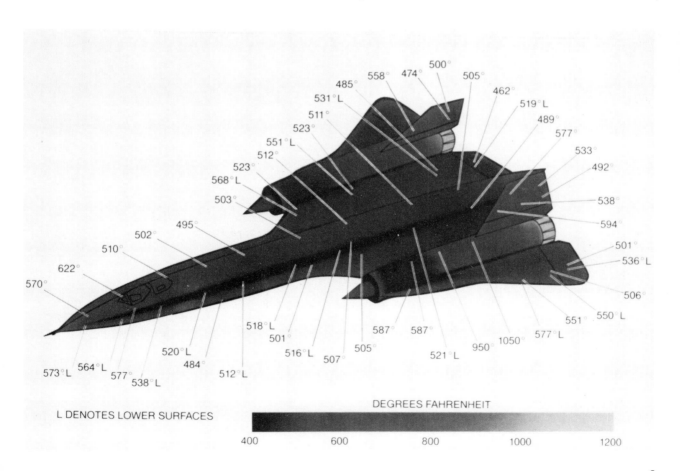

L DENOTES LOWER SURFACES

DEGREES FAHRENHEIT

400   600   800   1000   1200

89

An engine nacelle ring being processed in the machine shop using an automatic-tape milling tool (in the foreground) (Lockheed-California)

mounted reconnaissance sensors. With fairings smoothing the chine contour into the fuselage, the elongated cross section reduces radar cross section. This 'blended body' concept was designed into the F-12 series from its inception and as such represents the first application of Stealth technology.

Manufacture

Thermodynamic factors have influenced design and construction of the SR-71 family to a greater extent than on any other airplane flying today. Even the X-15 research aircraft, although nearly twice as fast as the SR-71, maintained maximum speed for only a few minutes on each flight. Sustained operation in this extreme temperature environment, meant lavish use of the advanced titanium alloys which account for 93 per cent of the aircraft's structural weight. The decision to use these materials was based upon the following considerations:

1. Only titanium and steel could withstand the operating temperatures encountered.

2. Aged B-120 titanium weighs only half as much as stainless steel per cubic inch, but has a similar tensile strength.

3. Conventional construction was possible using fewer parts.

4. High strength composites were not available in the early sixties. (Plastic was developed by the Skunk Works but it was not used for primary structure).

The sustained high heat soaking of the SR-71 took airframe temperatures to 570°C. This precluded the use of aluminium as the basic structural material. The decision to use titanium represented a milestone in the continuing evolution of aviation materials, and led to the invention and perfection of many new and different airframe assembly procedures. Manufac-

SR-71s under construction in the main assembly building at Burbank in October 1964 (Lockheed-California)

turing equipment had to be designed and built from scratch.

The particular titanium selected was B-120VCA (Ti-13V-11Cr-3A1), which can be hardened to strengths up to 200 Ksi. It also has a cold formability potential that promised reduced fabrication costs. The ageing process initially required 70 hours to achieve maximum strength but, with careful processing techniques, this was reduced to 40 hours. Great care is taken to ensure that the alloy is not over-aged as this results in brittleness. Some of the early coupons fell fowl of this, and shattered when dropped from desk height. Lockheed believed the cause was hydrogen embrittlement in their heat treatment process but, despite the close co-operation of their supplier, Titanium Metals Corporation, the case was not proven. The problem was eventually resolved after Lockheed replaced their entire acid pickling facility with a unit identical to that used by TMC.

Lockheed also set up a rigorous (and expensive) quality control programme. For every batch of ten or more parts processed, three test samples were heat treated to the same level as those in the batch. One was then strength tested to destruction, another tested for formability, and the third held in reserve in case reprocessing should be required. With more than 13 million titanium parts manufactured, data is available on all but a few.

Titanium is not compatible with chlorine, florine or cadmium, and this has created difficulties. A line, for example, drawn on a sheet of titanium with a Pentel pen will eat a hole through it in about 12 hours. Not surprisingly, all Pentel pens were checked in. Early spot welded panels produced during the summer had a habit of failing, while those put together in the winter lasted indefinitely.

Through diligent detective work, it was discovered

The fuel system test rig checked flow rates over a wide range of climb/descent angles (Lockheed-California)

that to prevent the formation of algae in the summer, the Burbank water supply is heavily chlorinated. All titanium parts were subsequently washed in distilled water. Bolt heads began dropping from installations—caused by tiny cadmium deposits left after cadmium plated spanners had been used to apply torque. As the bolts were heated (in excess of 320°C) their heads dropped off. All cadmium plated tools were removed from tool boxes.

To prevent parts going undergauge whilst in the acid baths, metal gauges two thousandths of an inch thicker were used. When the first A-12s were built, a drill bit would cut just 17 holes before it was ruined. By the end of the programme Lockheed ADP had developed drills that would bore 100 holes and then be successfully resharpened. Thousands of feet of wing extrusions were used on the Blackbird family, at an initial manufacturing cost of $19.00 a foot; this too was later reduced to $11.00 a foot.

To form titanium sheetmetal a large press was designed and developed by ADP, under Air Force contract, and built by Phillis. A furnace was built to preheat steel dyes to 760°C. The hot dyes were then moved to a sizing press and kept hot electrically. An hydraulic press applied pressure to the titanium parts, folding them at a constant pressure and temperature over a processing period of 15 minutes. The formed parts were then rolled out of the press, removed from the dyes and allowed to cool before further processing.

Lockheed awarded the Wyman Gordon Company a $1 million contract to fund a research programme into methods of forming complex structural pieces such as the gear legs and engine nacelle rings. The result was a unique hot forging process which utlilises a 50,000 ton press to force the titanium to the desired shape. Tape controlled milling machines, equipped with Lockheed designed high-speed cutting tools, were used to machine such items. ADP even developed a new cutting fluid which, as well as eliminating the corrosive effects of many similar fluids, permitted metal removal at double the normal rates. The parts were then pickled and cleaned, a pre-assembly inspection carried out and the relevant segments assembled on spot welding machines. To prevent oxidization, which in titanium leads to hydrogen embrittlement, welding was conducted in specially constructed chambers with a neutral, nitrogen gas environment.

One test undertaken studied thermal effects on large titanium wing panels. An element approximately 4 ft × 6 ft (1.2 × 1.8 m) was heated to the computed heat flux expected in flight and resulted in the sample warping into a totally unacceptable shape. The problem was resolved by manufacturing chordwise corrugations into the outer skins. At the design heat rate the corrugations merely deepened by a few thousandths of an inch and on cooling returned to their basic shape. Kelly Johnson says that he was accused of 'trying to make a 1932 Ford Trimotor go Mach 3', but added that 'the concept worked fine'.

Another problem to be overcome was that of thermal stress caused by severe temperature gradients between different structural elements. Consider, for example, three points on an aft, inboard wing section: the spar cap, located at the top of the spar, the spar web, at its centre, and the surface skin. Given a uniform start temperature of 27°C, at eight minutes after acceleration the spar cap temperature will be 77°C, the spar web 102°C and the skin 177°C. It takes a further 16 minutes before all three are within 8°C of each other. The problem, therefore, was how to attach a sheet of thin titanium skin to much heavier sub-structure without the former buckling or tearing. The Skunk Works applied the KISS formula—'Keep it simple, stupid'—and used a standoff type clip. Thus structural continuity was provided by creating a heat shield effect between adjacent components.

The reason behind the menacing black paint can be found in Kirchhoffs law of radiation. This states that a good absorber is a good emitter, and a good absorber is a black body. Since convective heating decreases with increasing altitude and radiation is independent of altitude, to take advantage of the radiation component when cruising above 70,000 ft (21,341 m), an aircraft needs a high surface emissivity. Iron ball black paint was to be the operational colour scheme for all the F-12 series, giving an emmissivity value of 0.93 compared to 0.38 for a bare titanium surface. The 15° to 30°C temperature reduction attained was considered worthwhile despite a 60 lb (27 kg) weight penalty. There were also tactical advantages: a black aircraft against an almost black sky (SR-71 cruise altitude) is difficult to see, and tiny iron balls said to be in the paint help dissipate electro-magnetic radiation, making the airplane difficult to locate with radar.

Another paint project, involving Ben Rich, the chief thermodynamicist, involved the national insignia. Rich was required to develop red, white and blue paint that would not tarnish with repeated heat soaks. Rich asked 'who'll be up there to look at them?' but the Air Force insisted and the job cost thousands of dollars.

But perhaps a more relevant problem for Ben and his engineers concerned the air conditioning system. The task involved producing a system for cooling air at up to 430°C to a temperature more useful for the job. A two-stage system was devised whereby the air, bled from the 9th stage of the compressor, is led first through a ram air bleed, air cooled and then through a fuel air cooler. The result is air conditioned air at −20°C which is supplied to the cockpit, where it maintains the steady state temperatures of 20°C to 30°C; ducted through the equipment, reconnaissance sensor and nose wheel bays, and, having reached a temperature of 60°C to 75°C, it is vented overboard via exit louvres. A pressure differential of 1 psi is maintained in the bays to ensure that the flow always vents out.

As fuel is burnt off, and the temperature of the remaining fuel rises, a system of smart valves is used. This directs hot fuel to the engines and cool fuel back into the tanks for environmental air cooling. The hot fuel is first used as a hydraulic fluid to activate the main and afterburner fuel nozzles before being injected into the fuel burners at over 350°C and 130 psi. It is of course no ordinary fuel, but JP-7, specifically designed by Pratt & Whitney Aircraft in conjunction with Ashland, Shell, and Monsanto for the F-12 series. It is a hydrocarbon fuel of low vapour pressure. As the fuel is burnt, gaseous nitrogen is fed into the fuel tanks to pressurize them and reduce the risk of inadvertant vapour ignition. The nitrogen is stored as a liquid in two 398 US gal (105 lit) dewars, approximately 2½ ft (0.7 m) long and 1½ ft (0.4 m) square, with well rounded corners. They are located either side of the front nose gear in the wheel well. Each time the SR-71 is air refuelled, the nitrogen gas in the fuel tanks is vented overboard. Range is governed by the number of times the SR-71 can be refuelled before the liquid nitrogen supply is depleted. There was talk of a third dewar being installed on selected aircraft to increase effective range, but it is not known if this work has been carried out.

With a high surface area to volume ratio tank sequencing dictates that, for thermodynamic reasons, fuel in the wing tanks is used first. Fuel tank sequencing is automatic and provides centre of gravity control by pumping fuel from one area to

another. An interesting side effect of fuel depletion is that the chines are pushed down. This is due to differential expansion between the top and bottom of the fuselage: fuel at the bottom of the tanks is keeping the underside cooler.

Development of a durable fuel tank sealant is an ongoing problem. Flying at high Mach and altitude, thermodynamic heating causes the aircraft to expand 3 inches in length despite ambient air temperatures of $-60°C$. The steady state airframe temperatures will all be in excess of $230°C$ and even a 15-minute deceleration and descent to 26,000 ft (7927 m) for refuelling will not reduce airframe temperature to anything like the outside air temperature of perhaps $-50°C$. One can imagine the effect JP-7 from a KC-135 tanker delivered at 5,000 lb (2278 kg) per minute and $-50°C$ would have on the silicon based sealant.

Sub-assembly of the SR-71 took place in various areas of the Skunk Works. Major sections of the fuselage and wing were fabricated and assembled in two halfs, a technique resulting in considerable savings of time and money. Before final assembly the inner wing was joined to the centre fuselage, followed later by the engine inlets.

A variable geometry supersonic inlet runs from a low pressure condition to a high pressure condition. The low pressure air exits at altitude. The inlet is propelled into this supply of gas at supersonic speed and, at the rear or engine face of the duct, ingested air is removed by the compressor section at a rate sufficient to maintain smooth flow. Fully retracted, the spike decreases the inlet cross section to slow the entering air and increase its pressure until the inlet throat is reached. A 'normal', or planer shock wave, is created at this point, as in a sonic venturi. With the air at subsonic speeds, the duct cross section is increased so that the air velocity decreases further and pressure increases uniformly until the engine face is reached.

With the platform operating at supersonic forward speed, the inlet is 'started' automatically by changing the cross section area of the inlet entrances (retracting the spike into the inlet), creating a 'normal' shock wave at the inlet throat (point of minimum cross section) and decelerating the air to about 300 knots (555 km/h) as it enters the engine face. Otherwise, air pressure continually increases during flow from front to rear of the inlet. With inlet pressures of 19 to 20 psi at altitudes where the ambient pressure is appro-

Anchored firmly to the ground, SR-71A 64-17980 is prepared for engine run-ups at Beale. The Buick V-8 start cart is on the left
(Paul F Crickmore)

ximately 0.4 psi (or less) the inlet produces a large forward thrust vector. The high efficiency of the concept can be judged from the table below which lists the percentage measure of overall thrust produced by each component while operating with maximum afterburner.

Mach no	Inlet	Engine	Ejector
2.2	13%	73%	14%
3.2	54%	17.6%	28.4%

If the throttles are eased back to the minimum afterburner position at Mach 3.2, the engine would actually drag on its mounts. Further power reduction below military power results in no propulsive thrust on the aircraft. The engine is therefore designed to be flown with afterburner at Mach 3.2, with engine thrust to weight ratio stabilizing at about 5.2:1. Fuel consumption is approximately 8,000 US gal (30,303 lit) per hour.

The high pressure differential between the ambient air and that produced in the inlet will, should the uniform flow in the duct become unstable or broken down, cause problems. In this 'unstart' condition, pressure in the duct at the engine face drops in an instant to 4 or 6 psi—that's a comparable drop in a manifold pressure on a reciprocating engine of from 36 inches to 8–12. With the engines mounted at mid-semi span to remain outside the fuselage flow, the resultant drag and accompanying aerodynamic excursion can be violent. The aircraft yaws viciously in the direction of the unstarted engine and has a tendency to roll off one wing. Crews have been thrown about with a force sufficient to dash their helmets against the cockpit walls. Under such conditions an automatic inlet restart sequence is initiated.

Unpleasant unstarts certainly are, and in the beginning the airplane suffered from far too many. This led to the term 'aerodynamic disturbance', or 'AD', being coined. Why the change? Imagine trying to explain the reason for a mission abort to a general like this: 'Sir, the pilot experienced a series of hard unstarts at Mach 2.6 and could not proceed.' 'Nuff said!

Mice are to be found in the back of the inlet ducts, clinging rigidly to the spike centrebody. These small streamlined protuberances act like vortex generators. Introduced to cure a bad diffusion rate, they change the area of distribution and thereby improve recovery.

Working on the Oxcart programme and the SR-71 in conditions of extreme secrecy, unable to talk to anyone about the programme except those directly associated with it, produced a restrictive working environment. To ease some of the strain, Lockheed engineers rechristened certain aircraft assemblies. The free floating, trailing edge flaps at the end of the nacelles, used to help shape the exhaust plume, were referred to as 'tailfeathers'. Less obviously, 'onion slicer' was used to describe the forward bypass and 'cabbage slicer' the aft bypass. Such terms were not tolerated for long and a directive was soon in circulation instructing that henceforth correct terminology would be used and not cabbage slicer, onion slicer etc.

Pratt & Whitney produced the superlative JT11 D-20 engine (designated J58 by the military), for the project. It was developed from a 1956 design (designated J58-P2 and commissioned by the Navy

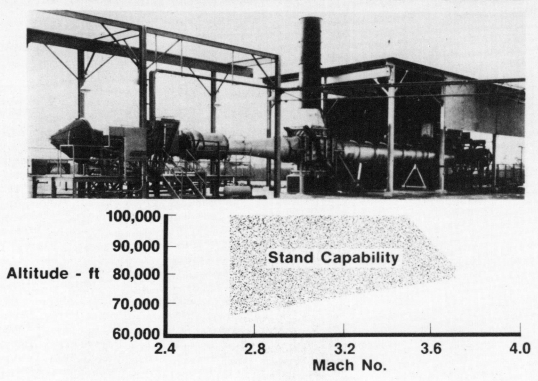

HEATED ENVIRONMENT TEST STAND

AV 218314
810604
gn1-449

for an attack aircraft with a required dash capacity of several seconds at speeds of up to Mach 3) and utilized ram compression to suppliment the compressor's moderate pressure ratio. Exhausting through a convergent-divergent exit nozzle, it was expected to provide 26,000 lb (11,818 kg) of thrust with afterburner at sea level.

But the project was dogged by problems and escalating costs and eventually abandoned by the Navy. But 700 hours of full scale testing had been completed, a fact that must have influenced Kelly Johnson and Pratt and Whitney's chief designer, William H Brown, in their decision to develop the engine for the A-12, a decision endorsed by the US Air Force and CIA despite projected costs of nearly $600 million.

The design team was headed by Brown and included Don Pascal, Norm Cotter, Dick Coar and Ed Esmeier; while William Gorton, the Pratt & Whitney Florida general manager, provided positive leadership and helped promote a good rapport with both Lockheed and the customer.

The resurrected engine was dove-tailed into the vast operating envelope of the A-12/SR-71 by employing a bleed bypass concept conceived by

A J75 engine (the original powerplant of the A-12) was employed to test the J58 at high operating temperatures (Lockheed-California)

TOP RIGHT
Bill Brown's masterpiece—the Pratt & Whitney J58 turbojet. Three of the six engine bypass ducts are visible in the middle and, moving to the front of the engine, variable-angle intake guide vanes are a feature of the turbine blades. The J58 produces 32,500 lb (14,742 kg) of thrust with afterburning
(Pratt & Whitney)

BOTTOM RIGHT
A J58 engine on its transport dolly (Paul F Crickmore Collection)

With the right engine fully ignited, the start cart can be removed (right). This picture was taken inside one of the barns at Beale AFB (Lockheed-California)

Robert Abernethy. This involves bleeding air from the fourth stage of the nine stage axial flow compressor, through six bypass ducts operating at low compression ratios. This decreases airflow across the rear stages of the compressor assembly, whilst increasing it in front, thereby preventing the rear stages choking with the high axial velocity air flow, and the front stages stalling from low mass airflow. To further minimize stalling the front stage of the rotor blades at low engine speeds or 'off design' speeds, a preceding assembly of hydraulically operated, variable angle inlet guide vanes (IGVs) are used. The scheduling of IGV shift is either automatic, through an actuator sensitive to compressor inlet temperature and engine RPM, or manuall controlled by the pilot. The automatic shift point was changed several times during the flight test programme. Due to hysterics in the automatic control, the shift did not always occur at the same speed during deceleration. Also the engine stall margin turned out to be rather slim at the idle schedule so,

following a rash of single and double flame outs during descent and deceleration, a procedure of manually controlling the IGV shift during this phase was adopted.

At designed cruise speed, with compressor inlet temperature at 425°C, turbine inlet temperature is 1100°C. Fabrication and materials technology to withstand such awesome temperatures, presented Brown and his design team with one of the greatest challenges. Joseph Moore, a materials engineer at the Florida Research and Development Center (FRDC), perfected the production of astrology discs for the J58's first and second stage turbines. Moore and his team also developed a new high temperature alloy for turbine blades and a manufacturing process to roll large sheets of Waspaloy for the fabrication of J58 cases.

Temperature related problems led to the development of a high temperature combustion fuel. JP-7 removes the risk of fire brought about by high skin temperature of the 'wet' fuel tanks. Having no lubricity, a small amount of fluorocarbon was added, enabling the fuel to serve as a hydrolic fluid for activating airframe and engine pump servos. Tetraethyl borane (TEB) is used to ignite both the main engine and afterburner as normal high energy ignition plugs are not capable of producing the required temperature. Advantages gained with this system include no arching during ignition, and cooling requirements kept to a minimum. The disadvantage is a small tank of TEB is carried aloft to help engine restart in the event of a flameout. With no other method of re-ignition available, once the supply of TEB is exhausted either a single engine landing becomes necessary or it's 'bye-bye birdy'—the aircraft is not capable of making a dead-stick landing.

Fuel inlet temperatures can reach 350°C at the point of feed into the annular combustion chamber. From here the airflow progresses downstream to the single shaft, two-stage turbine. Having produced the power to drive the compressor and various accessories, turbine stream is mixed with most of the bypass bleed air from the compressor section, before reaching the afterburner fuel injection and stabilizer system. Exhaust gas temperatures, of up to 1750°C in this section progress to the ejector nozzle and are finally expelled.

At the start of deceleration and descent, the pilot maintains military power in order to observe cool-down restrictions on the engine. Too rapid a cooldown results in the compressor case being hit by the tips of the compressor blades and causes mechanical damage. Under certain emergency situations, however, the risk is accepted in order to minimize the time taken to reach habitable altitudes or a safe speed.

To enable the highly stressed turbine blades and nozzle guide vanes to carry out their arduous job and achieve satisfactory working without reaching the end of their useful creep life, the early J58 engines were equipped with a turbine inlet temperature (TIT) measurement system. Temperature instrumentation was supplied to the cockpit and TIT switches were provided to enable the pilot to make independent adjustments of his power lever position. Therefore, while at military or afterburner power setting, the main engine TIT could be adjusted to optimize engine/afterburner performance. But accurate measurement and control of TIT proved difficult and the engine instrumentation positioned ahead of the turbines was thought to present a real hazard in the event of the thermocouples becoming unglued. The system was consequently abandoned in favour of measuring and controlling exhaust gas temperature (EGT). With this system, if mechanical items came apart the pieces pass through the afterburner spray bars and out of the tailpipe with a minimum probability of catastrophic damage.

For the system to work in practice, the fuel control system had to operate in a stable manner while compressor inlet temperatures varied from subsonic lows of −40° to −60°C, to supersonic highs of hundreds of degree Centigrade. As early systems could not be manufactured to remain 'flat', the EGT switches provided a way to bias the fuel controls. But the amount of bias effective at engine start depends on the amount of trim cranked into the engine while at military power during the previous flight. It was soon found that throttle advancement for takeoff could, and did, result in some very strange EGTs. The pilot might find himself groping for trim

switches in order to control EGT over or under temperature conditions while accelerating along the runway with full afterburner. To avoid this 'trim runs' were instituted at the head of the runway, with wheels chocked, and the engines individually brought up to military power and EGT adjusted before beginning the takeoff run. The adjustment was usually on the low side of the desired range so that if trim changed during takeoff, it probably would not travel too far beyond the limit before the pilot was in a position to devote some of his attention to the matter. Trimming too low was not desired either, as significant loss of afterburning thrust would result. With time, and along with other changes, Pratt & Whitney modified the EGT gauge by feeding in an engine inlet temperature signal for automatic engine trim. But the digital EGT readout was retained, as was the manual override trim switches in case of failure.

Afterburning is possible in turbojet engines because of the very lean fuel/air ratio they use to operate. Additional fuel can be burned in the tailpipe after the main engine has burned enough fuel to provide its share of thrust. But a rapid change in internal airflow—such as an unstart—will cause the TIT to rise many hundreds of degrees in a very short time unless the fuel control is reduced. If the fuel/air mixture is not deriched—either by automatic operation of the fuel control or by manual control of the power lever (throttle)—the engine may be destroyed in seconds. Derichment is energized when a high rate of increase in the EGT, substantially above the normal limit, is detected. The deriched (decreased) fuel flow remains in effect until reset automatically or manually.

Early in the design of the A-12, a bet was made between Kelly Johnson and Bill Brown as to who could design the best ejector system for the aircraft. It was agreed that the loser would pay for the wind tunnel tests on the unit, which Brown estimated at $12,000. Pratt & Whitney won, and true to his word, a cheque from Kelly Johnson arrived. Seeing a wonderful opportunity to set tongues wagging, Brown acquired a yachtsmans' outfit complete with navy blue blazer and cap, and had his photograph taken standing in front of Bill Gortons 41-ft (12.5-m) boat. On the picture sent to Johnson he wrote 'Thanks for the cheque'. The picture hung on the wall of the Lockheed executive office for years.

All classified projects undertaken by the Skunk Works are known as 'blackworld' programmes. Extraordinary lengths are taken to hide what is going on. The President and probably less than a handful of government officials are privy to the Skunk Works inner sanctum. Money is paid through dummy companies and materials delivered to warehouses rented by Lockheed under bogus names. One such 'company', used Kelly Johnson's initials and became the C & J Corporation. There were dozens more, and many are still being used. Key personnel were given

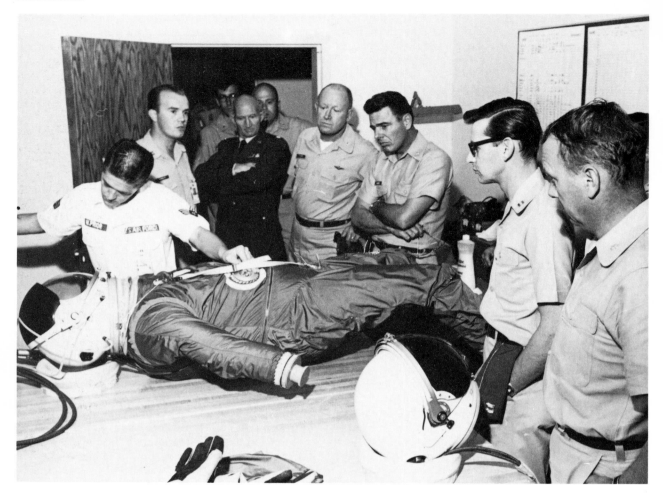

Sgt Bill Prior demonstrates inflation of the S901J inner
suit before an interested audience
(Paul F Crickmore Collection)

code-names, (Ben Rich was called 'Ben Dover'—a famous comic). Mail is sent to the airport at Burbank and collected by courier later. Drawings were not stamped—given an opportunity people will always read anything stamped SECRET.

The David Clark Company of Worcester, Massachusetts are responsible for manufacturing the life supporting pressure-suit. At high-altitude many physiological problems arise which, if left unchecked, would kill the crew in minutes. These problems are summarized on the right.

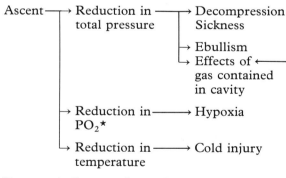

Ascent ──→ Reduction in ──→ Decompression
total pressure Sickness

──→ Ebullism
──→ Effects of ←
gas contained
in cavity

──→ Reduction in ──→ Hypoxia
$PO_2\star$

──→ Reduction in ──→ Cold injury
temperature

Descent → Increase in total pressure ──────
$\star$: PO_2 = partial pressure of oxygen.

Other problems may also arise as a result of entry into this abnormal environment, which can interfere with the crews normal vision and spatial orientation. Finally, flights at such high altitudes may be expected to have some psychological effect.

Hypoxia is the most serious risk facing the crew. This results from the drop in the partial pressure of oxygen (PO_2) on ascent. If unprotected at 25,000 ft (7622 m) for example, there are progressive cardio-respiratory and neurological effects because of the fall

An SR-71 with the chine panels removed to reveal its sideways-looking airborne radar (SLAR) antenna. This photograph was taken nearly 20 years ago and the Blackbird fleet is currently believed to have a high-resolution Goodyear synthetic aperture radar (SAR) system
(Paul F Crickmore Collection)

in PO_2, and individuals may suffer such symptoms as euphoria, personality change, loss of judgement, and impaired memory. Semi-consciousness and unconsciousness follows, with death resulting four to five minutes later. The symptoms compress and accelerate above 45,000 ft (13,720 m) with consciousness lost in 15–20 seconds, and death following four minutes later.

Decompression sickness (DCS) develops above 25,000 ft (7622 m), acquired with increasing rapidity and severity the higher the altitude DCS results from the evolution of nitrogen gas bubbles from body fluids as the ambient pressure falls, (much like the bubbles generated in a carbonated drink bottle when the lid is removed). Joint pain (the 'bends'), chest pain, skin itching and neurological manifestations may develop alone or together, the latter being the most serious and can be fatal.

The gas-contained cavities of the body—lungs, the gut, the middle ears and the sinuses—obey Boyles Law when subjected to pressure changes (in the constant temperature environment of the body), thus gas will increase in volume on ascent and contract on descent. Most of the problems associated with these changes are self-righting via the bodies orifices. But gas within the small bowel is not free to escape and its expansion can cause abdominal pain. This effect is reduced by a controlled diet providing a minimum of residual intestinal gases, fed to the crew before flight. Considerable pain can also arise during descent if air is unable to re-enter, and thereby equalize pressure in the middle ear cavities and sinuses. Crews undergo medicals before flight and are not allowed to fly if they have a throat infection or a slight cold.

Were the air crew to be subjected to the ambient air temperature of $-52\,°C$, prevailing at 80,000 ft (24,390 m) they would without doubt risk local or general cold injury (frostbite and hypothermia respectively.)

To protect the crew the cockpit is pressurized and pressure suits are worn. Within the cockpit, pressurization is allowed to rise from sea level to

8,000 ft (2439 m) and then remains constant to 25,000 ft (7622 m). At these altitudes the pressure of the ambient air falls from 10.9 psi to 5.9 psi respectively, resulting in a pressure differential of 5 psi. This maximum figure is then maintained by the airplane's pressurization system throughout its flight profile. It ensures that the hull of the aircraft is not subjected to unduly high pressure gradients to keep construction weight down. But it means that the crew of the SR-71 must wear full pressure suits in order to survive; Air Force Regulation 60-16 requires that pressure suits be worn when flying above 50,000 ft (15,244 m).

The current pressure suit, the S1030, features a number of improvements over the old S901J suit used until 1974. Made by the David Clark Company, it is produced in 12 sizes, utilizes state of the art fabric materials and hardware, and incorporates a number of new design features. Its four layers consist of an outer coverall of Dacron (a form of terylene) which is durable, tear and fire resistant and coloured 'Old Gold'. A restraint/joint layer holds the suit together through restraint lines and acts as a pressure boundary. A third 'Bladder' layer performs a function similar to that of the inner tube in a tyre, and is made of polyurethane. The final Inner Scuff layer of lightweight Dacron protects the bladder layer from scuffing against other clothing and the urine collection device. An optional thermal garment can be worn inside the suit, but this is usually discarded in favour of more comfortable long cotton under-wear.

The suit is built to assume a seated position when pressurized; this aids cockpit mobility, but limits upright manoeuvrability. Entry is accomplished through a zipper enclosure, which extends from the crotch, under the torso, and up the back to the neck. Gloves complete the pressure seal and are attached via wrist hinges. The gloves are made with an outer layer of Dacron, with leather palms and a dipped rubber bladder inside. When the suit is under pressure, the palm of the gloves balloon and so there is an adjustable palm restraint running across the knuckles and the back of the hand. The gloves come in 13 sizes.

The boots feature heel retraction strips, which are connected by cable to the ejection seat on entry to the cockpit. The complete pressure suit system costs in the order of $30,000 a copy, and lasts between 10–12 years, undergoing a complete overhaul every five years, and a thorough inspection every 90 days or 150 hours.

The other essential ingredient in the life support system is, of course, the ejection seat. It is a modified Lockheed C-2 seat, originally designed for the F-104, and designated the Lockheed ADP SR-1 or F-1, stabilized ejection seat. Above is a typical ejection sequence at an altitude below 15,000 ft (4500 m).

$T = 0.0$	Initiate ('D' ring pull).
	Canopy jettison
	Shoulders and feet powered back.
$T + 0.3$ sec.	Catapult ignites.
$T + 0.5$ sec.	Motor deploys drogue
	Seat is off the rails
	Rocket catapult ignites.
$T + 0.7$ sec.	Drogue chute is full open and seat is stabilised.
$T + 1.1$ sec.	Rocket thrust is exhausted
	Seat decelerates.
$T + 1.7$ sec.	Man-seat separation occurs.
	Lap belt releases
	Shoulder straps cut
	Front cables cut
	D-ring cable cut
	Main parachute arms
$T + 1.9$ sec.	Main chute is deployed.
$T + 2.0$ sec.	Upper bridles of drogue chute are cut.
$T + 3.4$ sec.	Main chute is full open.

Above 15,000 ft the functions are the same, but the pressure suit is inflated to protect the individual against the pressure differential (described earlier) and retained in the seat. At 1.7 secs, the aneroid controlled separation initiators are armed, and the lower bridles of the drogue chute are cut. On reaching 15,000 ft the aneroid unblocks, seat separation occurs and the sequence continues.

Avionics

Avionics fit for the Lockheed SR-71 and its forerunners can be broken down into five principle areas of interest. The main operational categories are navigation equipment, communications equipment, mission sensors and data displays. A large proportion of the avionics fit forms part of flight control system, which is a fundamental part of the aircraft itself. First the navigation equipment. Tacan is a widely used radio navaid that provides measurements of the aircraft distance and bearing from a ground radio station. It is used extensively in military service, and while it is adequate for rendezvous tasks in friendly circumstances it is of little use during a mission over hostile terrain.

A self contained en-route navigation system, which

TOP RIGHT
An interchangeable radar nose section for the SR-71 on its custom-made trolley
(Paul F Crickmore Collection)

BOTTOM RIGHT
An interesting cross-section of the SR-71 minus its nose
(Paul F Crickmore Collection)

The blending effect of the chine on the fuselage cross-section helps to reduce the aircraft's radar image. Both the front canopy and the RSO's side window are masked during respraying
(Paul F Crickmore Collection)

enjoys a high degree of accuracy, without recourse to external radio navigation facilities, is a prerequisite for an aircraft of this type. An inertial navigation system (INS) is the natural choice for the SR-71, in view of its covert reconnaissance activities. A unit supplied by Northrop is used, and is believed to have demonstrated a position fixing accuracy of 1.0 n.ml/hour or better. Full control functions are bestowed upon the RSO, with perhaps only limited access to the INS given to the pilot. The remote unit is rigidly mounted as it is also a primary source of atitude and heading reference information. The controller units are also likely to have display capability, with the INS being integrated with the primary flight instruments.

Position update capability for the INS is provided by astro tracking. With 52 stars programmed into the units memory, a gimbal mounted platform continually tracks at least three celestial bodies at one time through a round port hole located on top of the fuselage between the RSO's position and the refuelling receptacle. Using this information in conjunction with a time datum supplied by a chronometer, accurate to within five milliseconds, a computer produces continual position updates from anywhere in the world, day or night, of better than 1,000 ft (305 m) in 10 hrs! This system is considered by many to be one of the most outstanding accomplishments of the programme.

Communications equipment: UHF radios are used for all normal communications during the non-covert phases of a mission. Supplied with an ACR-50 controller unit, it is located on the right console in the front cockpit and duplicated in the back. Military radio sets can be converted to 'secure speech' operation by adding extra equipment to code transmitted data, and to decode received data.

Located behind the Tacan controls in the right console of the front cockpit is the ATC transponder or IFF, which can operate in several different modes. The SR-71 uses Modes A and C. Mode C is hooked up to supply height readout information to ATC. This mode is suppressed by the RSO as the aircraft climbs through 60,000 ft (13,300 m), to ensure that civilian radar cannot monitor altitude performance. Mode A helps to provide identification to friendly air defence networks on arrival at an entry gate, on leaving, and more especially, re-joining friendly airspace. The device is turned off near the

A rear view of the detached radar nose of an SR-71 (Paul F Crickmore Collection)

reconnaissance collection area.

Although it has yet to be acknowledged officially, there is every reason to believe that microwave datalink equipment has been installed to provide real time reconnaissance capability.

Mission sensors can be broken down into three distinct categories; optical, radar and electronic support measures (ESM).

In the early days of the programme, the SR-71 had cameras for four different functions. A palletized camera nose houses a split scan optical barrel camera for horizon-to-horizon coverage.

Details of the cameras employed aboard the SR-71, especially their focal lengths, are not in the public domain. The sort of camera that one could expect to see would be something akin to the Fairchild F-924 or Itek KA-80. Both are equipped with a 24-inch focal length lens. Folded telephoto optics help to keep them reasonably compact. Supplying a roll rate signal to the camera enables it to compensate for roll rates up to 5 per cent per second. The Fairchild system features an f 4.5 lens with automatic focus and automatic control of shutter speeds. Roughly the size of a beer crate, the film capacity for the F-924 is 2,000 ft (609 m) and the overall weight, including film is 250 lb (114 kg). Dimensions for the KA-80 are much the same, with a film magazine capacity of 6,500 ft (1982 m).

Flying at altitudes often in excess of 82,000 ft (25,000 m) and with stand-off ranges upwards of 15 miles, the photographic needs of the intelligence community dictate that long focal length camera systems must be used to meet resolution requirements. The cameras carried on each flight provide this close-look capability. Palletized for tailoring to specific mission needs, the units are situated in the chines either side of the centreline, just forward of the wing leading edge and fuselage fillet. Positioned near the aircraft's CG they enjoy the most stable location available. A vertically mounted tracking camera was used until the mid-1970s to assist in fixing the precise position of each target. Today an airborne data annotation system (ADAS) slaved to the navigation system applies precise airplane position and attitude information to each shot.

Another task performed by the SR-71 is the collection of electronic reconnaissance.

The overall discipline of electronic warfare (EW) can be broken down into three categories; electronic support measures (ESM), electronic counter measures (ECM) and electronic counter counter measures (ECCM).

ESM can be described as actions taken to search, intercept, locate and analyse radiated elec-

The panel on the underside of the chine, together with a similar station on the opposite side, are believed to be where the superhetrodyne and Elint recorders are positioned (Paul F Crickmore Collection)

LEFT
The mid-west of the United States, as seen by the tracking camera of an SR-71 from approximately 80,000 ft (24,390 m)
(US Air Force via Paul F Crickmore Collection)

tromagnetic energy for the purpose of exploiting these in support of military operation. ESM is subdivided into electronic intelligence (Elint) and communications intelligence (Comint). The former is described in a Joint Chief of Staff Publication as 'technical and intelligence information derived from foreign, non-communications, electromagnetic radiations emanating from other than nuclear detonations or radioactive source'. Communications intelligence is described in the same publication as 'technical and intelligence information derived from foreign communications by other than the intended recipients'.

Elint is acquired after an enemy or potential enemy has used such a device and its 'print' recorded. Once obtained, a great deal of information can be gleaned.
1) determination of the carrier frequency
2) direction of arrival of the wave is measured—this leads to the position of the device being established
3) the type of device is determined (surveillance radar, gun laying radar, etc)
4) signal characteristics are obtained (pulse recurrance frequency), duration of pulse, polarization established, form of modulation etc.)

With this information an Elint library can be built up. Once this is done, steps can be taken to manufacture devices to counter the effectiveness of such equipment.

Passive radar warning receivers (RWRs) alert crews that weapon radars have been switched on. In the case of the SR-71, this leaves the RSO free to take the appropriate action if the safety of the aircraft or mission efficiency is jeopardized. In some circumstances this might require switching on an active device, that will jam or electronically counter an enemy's device.

The SR-71's Elint role is somewhat limited by the space available on the airplane, but it is known that within a chine bay there is at least one receiver and a video tape recorder. The aircraft may 'hoover up' a wide frequency band from perhaps 2-50 GHz or more.

An SR-71 on finals to land; in addition to the Elint panels and camera ports located on the underside of the chine, this aircraft also has the rarely seen optical barrel camera or 'OBC' nose
(Sgt G L Jones)

SR-71A 64-17967 on the ramp at Beale during a maintenance check. The bay for the palletized 'close look' camera is open near the centre of the aircraft
(Paul F Crickmore Collection)

Another view of '967 and the open 'close look' camera bay
(Paul F Crickmore Collection)

ECM fit on the SR-71 is of course highly classified. Even so, informed sources have stated that it does not carry chaff dispensers for generating a cloud of false radar returns, or flares to act as decoys against heat seeking missiles. Active means of defence *are* used; evidence from the 1973 Yom Kippur War strongly suggests that the SR-71 carries amongst other things a highly effective means of deceiving surveillance radar. This would create confusion during the target distribution phase by generating single or multiple returns that possess the same signal characteristics as the SR-71.

When the RWR aboard an SR-71 intercepts signals from an enemy surveillance radar network, its onboard processor identifies the type of radar from its signal characteristics. This information is displayed to the RSO, who can interfere with that signal if required. In the case described above, a second or third target is produced, by transmitting a replica signal on the same frequency as the surveillance radar after a suitable time has elapsed. A false target is thereby produced on the operators display, some distance beyond the real target. Depending upon the sophistication of the system fitted to the SR-71, erroneous bearing information can also be generated for these false targets.

In the Soviet arsenal, there are few missiles that possess the speed, altitude and sophistication to engage an SR-71. The SA-5 and some of the new generation missiles are however thought to possess a threat—particularly if deep penetration of Soviet airspace ever became necessary. Flexibility of Soviet missile design is such that either a radar guidance or command radio guidance system may be employed on the same missile type. The performance of both systems may further be enhanced by incorporating an infrared terminal guidance system.

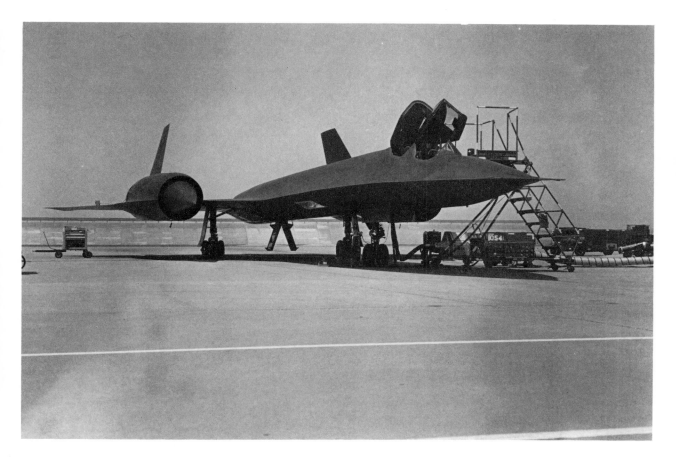

SR-71A 64-17964 in profile over the Sierra Nevada mountain range (Lockheed-California)

In the case of a radar guidance system being used, the SR-71 could use a system similar to that described earlier, with the false target signals changed to the same frequency used by the missile tracking radar. Other types of jamming that could be employed against such radars is continuous noise and pulse interferences, which offer an effective jamming 'curtain'. The last two methods of jamming exhibit certain disadvantages. They require a large transmitter, which an SR-71 might not be able to carry, and it is possible for ECCM to track a jamming source.

Automatic direction tracking using pulse-Doppler and monopulse systems is widely used today. A monopulse system enjoys a higher level of noise immunity than active jamming created at an isolated source. One of the few methods of defeating a pulse-Doppler system is velocity pull-off or range gate pull-off, depending upon the type of radar being deceived. As the missile or airborne radar carried by a fighter 'locks on' it 'throws' a velocity gate or range gate over the target and 'concentrates' on this return. The target then amplifies the signal and sends it back. This returned pulse is so big that it swamps the skin echo of the real target. As successive pulses rain upon the target a slight frequency change or a steadily increasing delay in the return pulse causes the gate to be moved progressively further away from the target. At a predetermined point the false signal is terminated. If the system has worked successfully, this leaves the missile or fighter 'dumped' a considerable distance away from the real target. The missile radar would have to drop into search mode and the whole process begin again, with time always against the interceptor. Misleading bearing information can be generated in a monopulse radar system by amplitude modulation of the signal.

The most impressive avionics system on the SR-71 is the flight control system. It is recognized that a prerequisite of all aircraft design work undertaken until 1972—when the YF-16 first flew—was that the basic air vehicle was aerodynamic and exhibited positive stability characteristics. That is to say, it would maintain straight and level flight in the absence of any control inputs or atmospheric disturbances. Positive long-term stability was acceptable, and some aircraft have divergent spiral stability characteristics, ie if an aircraft is correctly trimmed and left to fly itself, it will tend to drop one wing and eventually spiral down. However, positive short term stability is essential for an aircraft to remain controllable. This basic relationship between stability and control

Capt Joe Mathews demonstrating a simulated engine-out approach in 64-17974 during the 1984 Mildenhall airshow. Full afterburner from the right engine and hard left rudder is impressive to say the least; the right wing is held low to keep the aircraft flying in a straight line (Alan Hughes)

requirements certainly took a tremendous design team effort to achieve in the case of the Blackbird family.

The sheer scale of the SR-71 flight envelope makes incorporation of a full three-axis autostabilization system inevitable, and in the days of analogue computer technology the design task must have been formidable. Nevertheless, this is where designer Kelly Johnson achieved legendary success.

In a control configured vehicle (CCV) the advantages to be gained are a reduction in trim drag, reduction in control surface size and the suppression of control flutter. It is probable, although not officially acknowledged, that in some parts of the flight envelope the SR-71 depends on such a system. The SR-71 utilizes elevons and all-moving verticals. An elevon mixer assembly, located in the aircraft's tail cone, separates pilot stick motion into pitch and roll commands, which are then transmitted to the inboard and outboard elevons respectively. To reduce wing root bending moment, the outboard elevon is rigged 3° trailing edge up, in relation to the inboard elevon and the leading edge of the outboard wing section has 5° of conical camber. The outboard elevons provide approximately 85 per cent of the roll control via a torque tube system slaved to the inboard elevons. Both outboard and inboard elevons provide the same effectiveness in pitch control, and are limited to 24° trailing edge up and 11° trailing edge down. Roll control is limited to ±24° below 0.5 Mach and ±14° above 0.5 Mach, which provides good

*SR-71 pilot Maj Bob Behler models the David Clark
S1030 'gold suit', a type which became standard issue for
SR-71 crews from 1977. It comes with a GN-121394-03
flying helmet
(US Air Force)*

LEFT

Suitably secured, a Pratt & Whitney J58 turbojet is put through its paces— almost certainly generating its maximum thrust of 32,500 lb (14,740 kg). Apart from a string of characteristic shock-diamonds, the yellow-heat of the afterburner section is also noteworthy (Pratt & Whitney)

BOTTOM LEFT

SR-71A 64-17958 plugged in to the High Speed Boom of a Boeing KC-135Q tanker out of RAF Mildenhall, England, in June 1977. Article 2009, 64-17958 was the first A model delivered to the US Air Force (10 May 1966). Still active, '958 also established the current world airspeed record over a 15/26 km course when Capt Eldon W Joersz and RSO Maj 'GT' Morgan reached 2,193.167 mph on 27/28 July 1976 (Lt Col Bob Anselmo via Robert F Dorr)

TOP RIGHT

The morning after the night before: SR-71A 64-17980, callsign 'TROMP 30', taxies back to its hangar at Mildenhall shortly after 09:35 hr local time on 15 April 1986 after flying a photo-reconnaissance mission over Libya in the wake of Operation Eldorado Canyon (Colin Johnson)

ABOVE RIGHT

SR-71A 64-17960 outside its barn at Beale AFB, California, where the Blackbirds of the 9th SRW roost G Luxton

RIGHT

Streaming vortices, SR-71A 64-17971 lands at Mildenhall as a somewhat slower Lockheed product, a 'Europe One' camouflaged C-141 Starlifter, looks on in the background. (Lindsay Peacock)

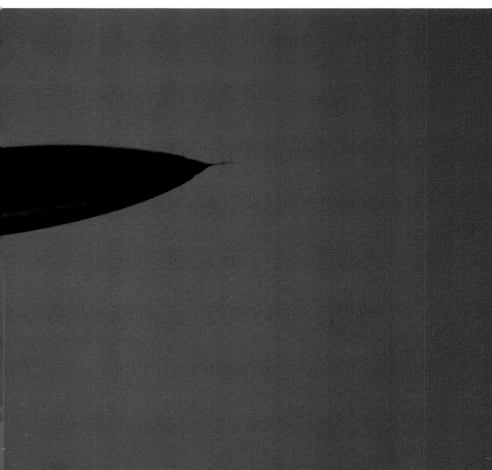

TOP
A more recent photograph of SR-71A 64-17958; the aircraft is in landing configuration prior to recovery at Beale (US Air Force via Robert F Dorr)

LEFT
Spectators at the 1986 Mildenhall Open Day were treated to this spectacular sight. Budding aerodynamicists will probably appreciate the flow pattern of the vortices; the flames eminating from the right-hand engine were caused by an excess of fuel after a 'squawk' developed on afterburner selection. The aircraft was in no danger (Ray Sumner)

TOP LEFT
SR-71B 64-17956 is the only surviving B model two-seat pilot training aircraft. Beale AFB is visible in the background
(US Air Force)

LEFT
SR-71A 64-17976 is scrutinized after landing at Kadena on 11 July 1977
(Toshiyuki Toda via Robert F Dorr)

ABOVE
Mean. Moody. Magnificent. SR-71A 64-17979, callsign 'OIL 54', pictured minutes before receiving takeoff clearance for an 07:30 hr departure from Mildenhall in 1984
(Paul F Crickmore)

A selection of patches worn by SR-71 crews

Also pictured on page 112, this is 974's simulated engine-out display at Mildenhall—an enthusiastic crowd lapped it up. Mathews' RSO was Capt D Curt Osterheld on this occasion
(Alan Hughes)

control and avoids roll coupling problems at higher Mach numbers. The all-movable vertical tails are limited to ±20° below 0.5 Mach and ±10° above 0.5 Mach.

The two primary requirements for trim on the SR-71 are pitch for altitude control and yaw for engine out conditions. These functions are provided by control-stick mounted trim buttons. Roll trim and right-hand rudder trim is provided on the left front cockpit console forward of the throttles, with trim position indicators provided for all three axes on the centre instrument panel. In the event of a trim failure, a trim power switch is located directly ahead of the pilot's left knee. This cuts all power to the trim systems, which then allows the pilot time to isolate the rogue unit by pulling the appropriate circuit breaker.

At high-speed cruise the aircraft exhibits only marginal positive pitch stability and elevon deflection per unit stick deflection is kept low about the neutral stick position to prevent control divergence.

The irreversible control system is hydraulically powered by two independent systems. Input through the stick and rudder pedals is transmitted to the hydraulic activators via a dual cable system. A potentially severe problem on the SR-71 was the effects of cable slack caused by the wide temperature range experienced in the airframe. To counteract this possibility a material with a low expansion coefficient, Elgiloy, is used for the cable and tension regulators.

SR-71A 64-17964 was forced to divert into Bodo, Norway, en route to Det 4 at Mildenhall. '964 made it to Mildenhall on 16 August 1981 (callsign 'HUMP 44'), adorned with the title 'The Bodonian Express' (Paul F Crickmore)

To provide optimum handling qualities for primary flight functions the aircraft is equipped with an automatic flight control system (AFCS). This consists of a stability augmentation system (SAS), an autopilot and a Mach trim system.

At the heart of the SAS are pitch and yaw roll rate gyros. To protect them against the effects of the severe thermal environment, the gyros are installed in a sealed unit encased in a jacket filled with Stearic acid. This is further insulated by another jacket through which fuel is circulated for cooling. The complete assembly is located in a stable area, within a fuselage fuel tank.

Air-data system data and pitch rate schedule unit inputs are used to determine the desired amount of proportional pitch data damping and static stability throughout the flight profile and helps to ensure that only safe control stick inputs are implemented.

The positive directional stability of the SR-71 becomes very low at high Mach; this coupled with potentially violent yaw transients created the need for directional stability augmentation. Information from the air data system and the yaw rate schedule unit are combined to tailor lateral and static directional stability characteristics. In the case of an engine unstart the system applies 9° of rudder within 0.5 seconds.

Roll axis presented no severe problems. The authority limit of the SAS servo is such that even a hardover failure is not catastrophic. It is however, a dual system as it provides all lateral autopilot modes and requires an element of inbuilt redundancy.

The pitch and yaw SAS is triple redundant throughout. The servos for the pitch axis are two dual tandem series servos, each dual servo driving an inboard elevon. The yaw axis employs four series servos, grouped in pairs, with each pair driving a separate vertical. The dual sensors of the roll axis employs one complete channel to drive each inboard elevon.

The scheduling is derived from triple redundant differential pressure sensors and altitude switches. They function as a package, completely independent from the central air data computer. An additional mechanized backup pitch damper is provided in case of failure.

The triple redundancy SAS, utilizes two functional channels and a reference or 'monitor' channel. A majority voting unit disengages the 'disagreeing' channel, while following a second failure a total disengagement of that axis is made. Should a channel subsequently be found to be still functional the pilot can re-engage it by using a logic over-ride switch. Cockpit monitoring of the system is provided by a system of lights, presented on the functional select panel, on the pilots right console. Logic recycling is completed by pressing the illuminated button. Preflight check of the SAS logic and AFCS disengage function is initiated by activating a logic check out switch, located adjacent the functional selector panel.

Crew E-18, Lt Col Roy L St Martin and his RSO Lt Col Cecil Braeden came close to disaster during a training sortie when they experienced an SAS failure. Accelerating through Mach 3 and 72,000 ft (21,951 m) the primary stability augmentation system automatically disengaged. Recycling the system, St Martin determined that it had failed and that they were therefore flying on the single remaining system. While employing single SAS emergency procedures, the remaining SAS also became disengaged. Recycling the second system had no effect; aircraft control became marginal and several dangerous pitch transients were encountered. Under these extremely difficult conditions an emergency descent and deceleration was initiated to regain more control over the aircraft. St Martin managed to recover the aircraft without further incident.

Between Mach 0.2 and 1.5 the aircraft has neutral or unstable speed stability characteristics. To improve stickforce feel, whenever SAS augmentation is engaged, and the autopilot disengaged, the air-data computer processes Mach number inputs, which are fed to the trim actuator.

At high-Mach cruise, the SR-71 exhibits low to negative pitch stability which further decreases with increasing angle of attack. To prevent the aircraft pitching up and into a deep stall, a redundant automatic pitch warning (APW) system warns of the approaching condition via a stick shaker. Angle of attack and pitch ratio are compared with Mach number to provide this information. Both functional channels of the SAS are utilized to ensure a measure of pitch rate redundancy.

The air-data system comprises of a nose boom and an air-data computer. The nose boom features a compensated pilot static probe and an offset hemispherical head flow-direction sensor. The compensated pitot static probe senses impact pressure at its tip and static pressure at two sets of orifices. These provide pressure measurements for the air-data computer, inlet computers, and flight instrumentation. The hemispherical head flow-direction sensor gathers angle of attack and angle of sideslip data.

Until the late seventies the electro air-data computer converted pitot-static pressures into proportional rotary shaft positions, which were equivalent to static pressure and dynamic pressure. By translating total temperature into a shaft position, this analogue computer could, through a series of cams, gears, and gear differentials, transpose shaft rotations into data outputs. Such outputs included true airspeed, (TAS) pressure altitude, Mach number, knots equivalent airspeed (KEAS), and altitude rates of change, differences between Mach number and Mach number schedule; KEAS and KEAS schedule and KEAS bleed schedule as a function of Mach number.

The autopilot is a subsystem which, whilst undoubtedly reducing pilot work load, is not essential to maintain platform stability. Indeed the traditional parallel servo for autopilot modes is not necessary and therefore not employed on the SR-71. Using outputs from the air-data computer, the automatic navigation system and the flight reference system, it performs best at the design flight conditions. Summed with the SAS outputs, the autopilot outputs are applied to flight control activators to provide the following modes:

In roll axis, the roll autopilot provides three control modes, namely: altitude hold, heading hold, and automatic navigation. In the altitude hold mode, data is taken from the flight reference system, altitude reference signal, and roll rate gyro. In the heading hold mode, outputs are used from the flight reference system. In the automatic navigation mode, the autopilot ties in signals from its astro inertial automatic navigation system. Roll axis autopilot outputs are combined with roll SAS outputs and supplied to the elevon activators. The autopilot pitch axis provides five modes of control, namely: altitude hold, attitude hold, Mach hold, KEAS hold and Mach trim. Locked in these modes an automatic trim circuit functions. Flying on pressure altitude, the altitude hold mode uses signals from the air-data computers altitude and altitude rate of change outputs. Pitch rate gyro outputs are combined with the pitch attitude reference and static pressure to function in the attitude hold mode. The pilot can apply minor corrections to the pitch reference altitude by turning a small pitch control wheel. Mach hold mode uses Mach number error and Mach number rate of change signals from the air-data computer. Similarly, KEAS hold is provided from air-data computer signals of KEAS rate of change and KEAS error outputs, this enables a specific KEAS 'bleed line' to be flown during the cruise climb. Pitch axis autopilot and pitch SAS outputs are combined and transmitted to the elevon activators.

The SR-71 has an autothrottle system which is limited to the afterburning range. Working through the autothrottle computer which receives signals from the air-data computer and the flight reference system, commands are sent to the autothrottle servos, which control both engines symmetrically. Locked in either Mach number hold or KEAS hold, the system allows the airplane to be flown in either mode without a change in its longitudinal flight path.

The most critical control aspect of high Mach flight in the SR-71 is without doubt the inlet control system, which schedules the variable-geometry mixed-compression inlets. By manipulating the spike and forward bypass positions, stationing of the normal shock is controlled. If positioned too far to the rear of the inlet a severe efficiency penalty is incurred, and loss of range will result. With the normal shock too far forward, inlet instability can result in an unstart. Mach number, angle of attack, angle of sideslip and normal acceleration are fed to the control system. This system then provides two outputs, commanded spike position and commanded duct pressure ratio, both of which are based upon Mach schedules arrived at during flight testing and wind tunnel programmes. The commanded spike position is compared with the actual spike position signals. An actuator then translates the spike until the commanded position is achieved. In this way the necessary contraction ratio at each Mach number is maintained.

The duct pressure ratio is derived from the pitot pressure on the outer surface of the cowl and the static pressure in the inlet throat. The throat static pressure varies with positioning of the terminal shock. The forward bypass doors are used to position the terminal shock so that the measured duct pressure ratio matches the duct pressure ratio commanded by the inlet computer.

When aerodynamic disturbances cause the normal shock to move outside the inlet an unstart occurs. This is detected by the inlet unstart sensor, which responds by feeding signals to the automatic inlet control system. This then causes the forward bypass doors to open at maximum rate, to the full open position. If the spike is retracted by less than 15 inches it is moved fully forward. If it is further aft than 15 inches, it moves 15 inches forward. Both the bypass doors and the spike are then slowly returned to the correct duct pressure ratio and the scheduled command. To reduce the severity of the yawing and rolling motions inherent in a high Mach unstart, the inlets are cross tied above 2.6 Mach, and automatically switch the functioning inlet into restart mode. Manual positioning of the spike and forward bypass doors of each inlet can be achieved by the pilot if so desired. This is done with reference to Mach number display.

Digital technology has now replaced the Honeywell analogue air-data computer, autopilot autothrottle and inlet control systems. This new system is known as 'DAFICS'—digital automatic flight inlet control system. A major programme to improve performance, reliability, and reduce pilot workload on the aircraft, the contract was awarded to Honeywell in mid 1978, with the first production sets being installed on the operational fleet during mid 1983.

Utilising three Honeywell 5301 processors, this triple redundant system is designed to a fail safe specification. Its built-in test (BIT) capability can not only isolate a particular processor but, in some circumstances, identify and isolate a malfunction on a specific card.

DAFICS calculates spike and duct pressure ratio command values every 9 milliseconds and forward bypass control values every 2 milliseconds. By scheduling the inlet more accurately, this has led to fuel savings of the order of 10 per cent.

Chapter 5
SR-71 Operations 1
Semper Paratus

Forty miles north of Sacramento, the Habu's lair began life in October 1942 as US Army Camp Beale. The camp was named in honour of General Edward Fitz-Gerald Beale, founder of the US Army Camel Corps, and in those days it stretched over 80,000 acres. In early 1948 the US Air Force acquired the site and by General Order 77 of 27 November 1951, the Beale Bombing and Gunnery Range became Beale AFB and reduced to 40,000 acres and (later 23,000 acres). Between 13 April 1957 and August 1958 a 12,000 ft (3658 m) runway was constructed and a year later the airbase was handed over to Strategic Air Command.

By mid-1964 the air contingent at Beale was the 456th Bombardment Wing, comprising the 744th Bombardment Squadron, equipped with Boeing B-52s, the 903rd Air refuelling Squadron with Boeing KC-135s, and the 851st Strategic Missile Squadron (SMS) which had Titan 1 intercontinental ballistic missiles. The 851st SMS were destined for a short stay at Beale—the Blackbird was about to take over.

That summer, the shrouds were drawn back on the secret project when President Lyndon B Johnson made the following announcement on 25 July 1964.

'I would like to announce the successful development of a major new strategic manned aircraft system, which will be employed by the Strategic Air Command. This system employs the new SR-71 aircraft, and provides a long-range advanced strategic reconnaissance plane for military use, capable of worldwide reconnaissance for military operations. The Joint Chiefs of Staff (JCS), when reviewing the RS-70, emphasized the importance of the strategic reconnaissance mission. The SR-71 aircraft reconnaissance system is the most advanced in the world. The aircraft will fly at more than three times the speed of sound. It will operate at altitudes in excess of 80,000 ft. It will use the most advanced observation equipment of all kinds in the world. The aircraft will provide the strategic forces of the United States with an outstanding long-range reconnaissance capability.

'The system will be used during periods of military hostilities and in other situations in which the United States military forces may be confronting foreign military forces . . .'

Unveiling the aircraft in this manner during the 1964 presidential campaign (following Johnson's earlier announcement concerning the existence of the A-11) shot the blackworld programme to the forefront of political debate and aroused public curiosity. Notably, this was an election year in the US. Johnson's announcement clearly set out to flatten charges by Republican nominee Barry Goldwater that the administration had neglected the defensive needs of the country and that not a single significant aviation development programme had been initiated during the Democrats' (Kennedy & Johnson) period in office. Goldwater's response was to claim that the SR-71 was 'simply a modification of the A-11', which was initiated under President Eisenhower. Since political disagreements about aviation and national readiness are rife during election campaigns many believed that Johnson aided his run for a second term in office by revealing the SR-71 just when he did, and in the manner he did.

It is unclear to this day why Johnson referred to the aircraft as the SR-71. Lockheed designated the aircraft R-12, which later received the designation RS-71 for political upmanship, the initials standing for Reconnaissance Strike. Originally the aircraft would have been capable of the dual role functions implied in the title, and the 71 designation followed that of the North American RS-70 (later B-70) Valkyrie. Whether the transposition was a calculated blunder by Johnson may never be known. Shortly after the Johnson announcement the 851st SMS with its troublesome Titan 1s were informed that its operations at Beale were to be phased out over a ten-month period. In October 1964 the US Air Force announced that the new resident at the airbase would be the SR-71.

Northrop T-38 Talon serial 00581 is used as a companion trainer by SR-71 aircrew. The 9th SRW badge is displayed in the middle of the fin below a band of four Maltese crosses
(Paul F Crickmore)

An $8.4 million military construction programme was initiated almost immediately at Beale, leading to the installation of technical support facilities and 337 new Cape Hart housing units for the newcomers. Local Congressman Robert Leggit said that phasing out the Titan missile at Beale would lose 21 civilian and 576 military personnel, but the SR-71 created 2,300 military and several hundred more civilian jobs.

The official announcement of the new SR-71 unit was made on 14 December 1964 when General John Ryan, Commander-in-Chief of Strategic Air Command, revealed that the 4200th Strategic Reconnaissance Wing would be activated at Beale on 1 January 1965. Three months after the 4200th was formed a number of support squadrons were also activated within the new reconnaissance wing, including the 4200th Headquarters Squadron, the 4200th Armament and Electronic Maintenance Squadron, 4200th Field Maintenance Squadron, and the 4200th Organizational Maintenance Squadron.

The first two of eight Northrop T-38 Talon trainers arrived at Beale on 7 July 1965. These agile and impressive white trainers with their slim tandem cockpit layout were pressed into use immediately to provide selected SR-71 crews with local area proficiency flying and landing practice. Col Douglas T Nelson was appointed to command the new wing

since the first appointee, Col John A Des Portes was promoted to Brigadier General and given overall command of the 14th Strategic Aerospace Division which commanded Beale and other west coast SAC bases under 15th Air Force.

Shortly after 1400 hrs, on Friday, 7 January 1966, Col Nelson, with instructor pilot Lt Col Raymond L Haupt, delivered the first SR-71B (serial number 17956) to Beale. The pilot trainer version had been flown from Edwards AFB with an escort of two T-38s and made an impressive first flyby at the private reception ceremony. A second SR-71B followed soon after; steadily the A models (standard reconnaissance versions) began to arrive until late 1967.

Right from the start, the Strategic Air Command kept 'Senior Crown' (the code-name for the SR-71 programme) exclusive, restricting recruitment to SAC's 'select' and most experienced crew members

The Det 6 flight test team at Palmdale in front of T-38, serial 10363, and evergreen SR-71A '955. Left to right: Maj Bill Frazier (RSO, SR-71) Lt Col Cal Jewett (pilot, SR-71) Capt Jack Stebe (pilot, U-2) Maj 'GT' Morgan (RSO, SR-71) Lt Col Jim Sullivan (pilot, SR-71) and Lou Armbrecht (Lockheed crew chief) (via Paul F Crickmore)

from bombers and U-2s. Of the first ten pilots, five were ex-B-58 pilots, two came from the U-2 unit, and two were former B-47 pilots. Only one of the two from the US Air Force Test Pilots School remained in the programme. SAC had manned the initial cadre almost exclusively with internal resources of trusted crew members, a tradition that lasted nearly eight years.

In those early days crew selection requirements were virtually identical to those used for the contemporary selection of astronauts. A prospective pilot required at least 2,000 hr flying time, of which 1,500 minimum had to be as aircraft commander or instructor in jet aircraft.

Today slight medical defects might be waived for an SR-71 applicant, so it is not uncommon to find a Reconnaissance Systems Officer (RSO) wearing glasses. But such dispensations apart, entry to SR-71 crew status is not easy as the appropriate Air Force Regulations, June 1982 (Section B, Paragraph 33) testify.

1. Pilot: a) Possess at least 1,500 hr of jet time, of which 750 hours must be as aircraft commander.
b) A Regular Air Force officer or Reserve officer with less than 16 years total active federal military service.
c) Medically qualified to fly the SR-71.
d) Eligible for Top Secret clearance.

The requirements for an RSO are similar with the exception of sub paragraph 'a' which stipulates that the applicant should possess a radar-bombardier/navigation type-rating.

Meeting these requirements, and passing a battery of selection tests is only the beginning for a new SR-71 crew. Evolution of SR-71 training techniques during twenty years of operations have changed the overall programme little. A pilot begins with many hours of flying training in T-38s, or in an SR-71 simulator at Beale, and only after completion of these introductory measures is he allowed to take the controls of an SR-71B. Under supervision of an instructor pilot his first sortie is tame by the standards demanded on most active missions. It will normally last about two hours and be conducted entirely at subsonic speeds. The indoctrination will include between 15–20 minutes air-refuelling practice with a KC-135Q tanker and will include normal flight

manoeuvers and landings. The next couple of sorties extend to about three hours duration and involve more air-refuelling practice, supersonic flying, and practicing the long descent from very high cruise altitude. Several instrument and visual circuits of the traffic pattern are made with five or six touch-and-go landings. On the fourth flight, three hours spent flying at night consolidates total experience (today night flying does not begin until the pilot has over 50 hours on the aircraft). Finally, the fifth flight is a standardization 'check ride' of approximately three hours which evaluates the pilot's suitability for command and indicates if further training is necessary. Pilots who reach the second stage are teamed with their simulator-trained RSO for six further training sorties in an SR-71A to attain 'combat crew' readiness status. Most of these training missions last three to four-and-a-half hours each and include some night flying.

The pilot then faces a second 'check ride' in the simulator with his RSO, and with 'no holds barred'. The instructors now test the crew's ability to control serious inflight emergencies, which involves airmanship and crew co-ordination of the highest order. A

Col Doug Nelson, commander of the 9th SRW (second from right) takes delivery of the first SR-71B (64-17956) from Bob Murphy, plant manager at Palmdale, on 6 January 1966
(Lockheed-California via Bob Murphy)

TOP RIGHT
Col Doug Nelson accepts the 9th SRW's first SR-71A (64-17958) from Bob Murphy on 10 May 1966
(Lockheed-California via Bob Murphy)

RIGHT
SR-71A refuelling from a Boeing KC-135Q of the 100th Air Refueling Wing (ARW). A total of 56 KC-135As were modified to 'Q' configuration; 15 examples are 'partial Qs' which lack the full avionics kit. The JP-7 jet fuel carried by the KC-135Q is unique to the SR-71 family

PRECEDING PAGES
Taken on 27 May 1967, this historic photograph records the initial compliment of pilots and RSOs assigned to the 1st and 99th Strategic Reconnaissance Squadron (SRS). The barns for the SR-71s are on the left
(US Air Force)

SR-71B 64-17981 slides away from the tanker after an air refuelling exercise. The recepticle door is still open (Lockheed-California)

day or so later a longer inflight profile sortie is flown and the entire flight is thoroughly evaluated using all available monitoring data, including the highly detailed cockpit and flight data recorders. By final evaluation a pilot has logged about 30–35 hours in the SR-71A/B and nearly 100 hours in the simulator. His back-seater has flown slightly fewer aircraft hours but has amassed more in the simulator. The new crew is then declared 'combat-ready' and can be expected to fly a number of two-hour training sorties along the US West Coast, or three-and-a-half hour missions encompassing an entire circuit of the continental USA every week. Regular visits to the simulator are still mandatory and a crew must accumulate at least 100 hours in the SR-71 before they are cleared to fly on transoceanic missions.

On 25 June 1966 the 4200 SRW along with its component squadrons underwent an important official heraldic redesignation. Following the de-activiation of the 9th Bombardment Wing at Mountain Home AFB (a B-47 unit with one of the most important old unit designations) the 4200 was redesignated the 9th SRW, while the subordinate squadrons became the 1st and 99th Strategic Reconnaissance Squadrons (the 1st being the oldest unit in the history of US military aviation).

Training kicked-off in 1965 and as supersonic SR-71 flying hours were chalked up in the west, the US Air Force found itself receiving sonic boom complaints. In 1967 some of the figures were:

City	1960 pop	complaints	claims
Chicago	3,520,000	1580	128
Los Angeles	2,695,000	836	220
Dallas/ Fort Worth	1,150,000	208	27
Minneapolis/ St Paul	773,000	58	7
New Orleans	655,000	9	0
Atlanta	535,000	4	1
Indianapolis	530,000	103	13
Denver	115,000	115	23
TOTAL	10,388,000	2,913	419

Most of the claims were attributed to climbs and descents as SR-71s accelerated or slowed before and after air-refuelling or final descents, but the apparent nuisance factor caused Congress to instruct the US Air Force to curtail flights over large urban areas.

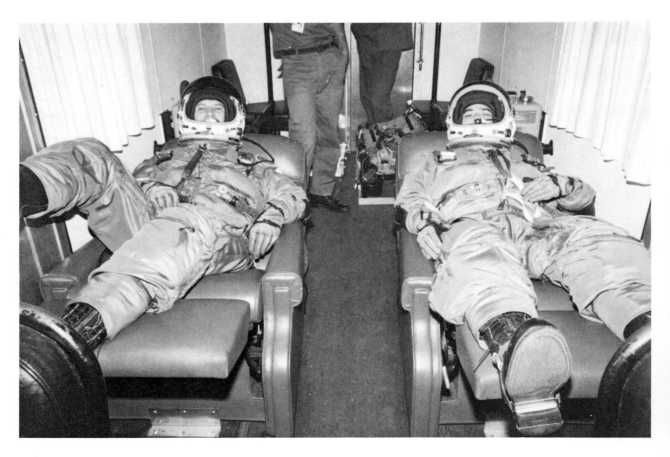

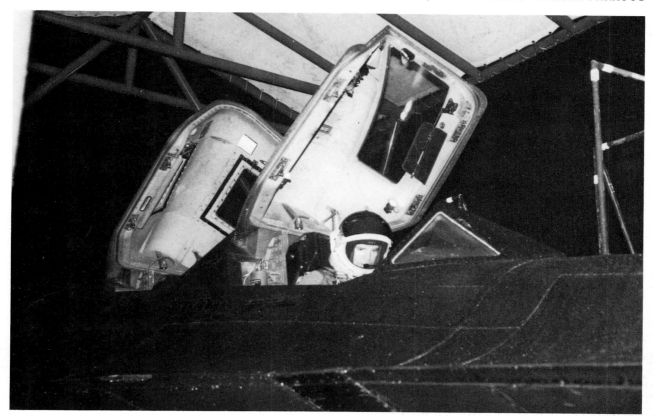

Maj Jiggins concentrates on his pre-startup checks prior to an early morning departure from RAF Mildenhall. Before the procedures were relaxed to take account of the SR-71's initial flight profile, the crew breathed 100 per cent oxygen shortly after suiting up
(Paul F Crickmore)

LEFT
The Buick V-8 start cart
(Kevin Gothard)

TOP LEFT
Major Bernie Smith fully kitted-out in his S1030 'gold suit'
(Paul F Crickmore)

BOTTOM LEFT
SR-71 crew Capt Rich Judson (left) and RSO Maj Frank Kelly in the PSD van before being driven out to the aircraft
(Paul F Crickmore)

Nowadays much of the training is conducted off the West Coast and tracks are varied to minimize annoyance.

To SR-71 crews the various flight paths are so commonplace that they are known as 'canned routes'. Many are named after mission planners' wives or friends and bear names such as Denise, Mary K, Nancy and Zelda. Denise is one of the longer routes, a so-called 'double looper', with two air-refuelling tracks and two long and high straight cruises. Another route, 'Nite Hound' is used at nighttime and also has two refuelling rendezvous tracks, while others called 'Tenderfoot' and 'Moby Dick' are shorter routes flown off the Californian coast.

A fully qualified crew will generally begin to

Maj Madison and RSO Maj Orcutt in SR-71A 64-17980
wait at the 'hammerhead' prior to lineup and departure
from Beale for a routine training flight on 14 June 1984
(Paul F Crickmore)

prepare for each of their two weekly training missions the day before they fly. Mission planners provide detailed plans and charts of the route to be flown and flight profile data, including computed fuel consumption rates and other details so the crewmen can familiarize themselves with the mission. The workload begins early on the day of the flight, starting more than three hours before takeoff. Flight plans are filed the day before and the crew obtain weather briefings, check Notams and airspace restriction data at flight operations. Soon after, they are briefed on the status of the assigned aircraft.

Standard Training Mission

About two-and-a-half hours before takeoff the crew goes to the physiological support building where they eat a high protein, low residue meal (usually steak and eggs.) Mission payload specialists ensure that the mission computer data tape is installed in the astro-inertial navigation system, and that the sensors are installed and programmed. Physiological Support Division (PSD) personnel checkout the cockpit environment control and life-support systems.

The next event for a crew is a routine medical check. Before every flight temperature and blood pressure measurements are taken, and eyes, ears, nose and throat conditions are checked to assure freedom from high altitude pressure related problems. A training mission can be cancelled for slight deviations from normal throat conditions, although important missions are backed up by a stand-by crew, who would have been shadowing the front crew up to this point and could easily be substituted.

One-and-a-half hours before takeoff the crew begin to dress. Like squires tending an armoured knight, two PSD personnel assist the crew into their full pressure suits, pressure gloves, astronaut helmet

The pilot of SR-71A 64-17974, Capt Rich Judson, waits for confirmation from a Lockheed maintenance engineer that the external inspection was 'squawk free'
(Kevin Gothard)

and special boots. The system is then inflated and checked for leakages and oxygen flow. After suit check, the crew is escorted to the PSD van where they can relax in the style of shuttle astronauts. Each crewman sits in a reclining armchair during the drive to the hangar or 'barn' which shields their aircraft from the weather, the heat of the sun, and the gaze of curious eyes. The crew then climb into the airplane. PSD personnel strap them in and connect their life support systems (oxygen and suit ventilation.) At this point the crew begin breathing 100 per cent oxygen to denitrogenate the blood stream.

Sixty minutes to go. The RSO calls out preflight checklist items, as the pilot readies switches for startup. Like most aircraft this takes about 20 minutes. Not less than half-an-hour before takeoff an engine is started. This can be achieved by employing an 'air-start' system or a ground-start cart. In the case of an air-start, compressed air is used to spool-up the main hp shaft to about 3,200 rpm (the same end is achieved by a ground cart via a mechanical drive which is cranked by two paired Buick V-8 automobile engines. With the big Buicks in full cry, the barn sounds like the pits at a race car meeting. At the appropriate engine speed the pilot moves the throttle forward to flight-idle. This causes the J58 fuel system to spray a small amount of Triethylborane (TEB) into the combustors, causing spontaneous combustion which lights the JP-7. The start procedure is quite distinctive from behind—a bright emerald-green flash occurs as the TEB oxygenates at very high self-combustive temperatures during the initial ignition process.

About two minutes later engine-powered hy-

draulics are checked and flying controls are tested for full free movement. After successful completion of the preliminary checks the second engine is also started. Either left or right engine can be started first. After both engines have quickly stabilized the crew works through another 15 minutes of checklist items before the flight can commence.

With flight clearance 'copied' the pilot commands the groundcrew to remove the chocks and to direct the SR-71 out of its lair. The pilot tests the brakes to assess their effectiveness and begins to follow a yellow guide line along the taxiway to the 'hammerhead' waiting ramp adjacent to the active runway entry point. As the aircraft stops, ground crewmen again chock the wheels before engine run-up tests. Each engine is independently run up to full military power as the pilot watches exhaust gas temperature (EGT) gauges. After satisfactory temperature stabilization, automatic engine trim is engaged to keep EGT within limits for maximum efficiency. The crew now wait five to ten minutes before takeoff commences. Once in a while, a last minute problem can fill this buffer period, but when all is reconciled runway clearance is granted about one minute before departure.

Cleared to lineup and depart when ready, the crew signals for the wheels to be unchocked. The pilot releases the brakes and The Lady moves purposefully to the takeoff point. About 20 seconds before the aircraft starts rolling, both throttles are advanced to full military power. The engine control system ensures that the inlet guide vanes, exhaust nozzle flaps, and a host of other invisible items are correctly positioned. After a quick check of engine instruments, the brakes are released and reheat power is engaged. The aircraft surges forward. Afterburner nozzles open fully as full power is reached, and a crackling pair of shock-beaded plumes stretch aft as the SR-71 races away from the start point. Nosewheel steering is light and positive and used up to about 120 knots (222 km/h) by which time lateral control is easily transfered to aerodynamic flow over the rudders. The aircraft will normally not be fully loaded and will weigh about 60 tons. In barely 20 seconds it accelerates from zero to 215 knots (398 km/h); the pilot then applies back pressure on the stick and the aircraft rears upwards like a proud cobra. At about 10° pitch angle the rotation reaches lift off attitude, and at about 230 knots (426 km/h) aerodynamic forces lift the SR-71 smoothly free of the runway.

The pilot immediately selects gear 'up' to prevent exceeding the 300 knot (555 km/h) limiting speed. With a vast amount of thrust available, the aircraft quickly accelerates to 400 knots (740 km/h) where pitch is smoothly increased and a rapid initial rate of climb of over 10,000 ft/min is established.

Departing Beale from runway 14, the aircraft turns gently to the left, towards Reno, about 100 miles (185 km) distant. The rate of climb is reduced and about four minutes after takeoff the aircraft is levelled at

SR-71A 64-17958 tucks away the gear after getting airborne from Beale. This aircraft established a world speed record over a 15/26 km course of 2,193.167 mph (3529.56 km/h) on 27/28 July 1976 (US Air Force via Robert F Dorr)

26,000 ft (7927 m) to approach a waiting KC-135 tanker to 'top-off' its tanks to the brim. It is standard procedure to start any mission with a 50 per cent to 66 per cent fuel load. Lighter weight allows a good margin of safety in the event of an engine failure on takeoff.

The tanker rendezvous is routinely practiced and executed in complete radio silence unless weather hazards intervene. Even on training flights radio calls are minimized as passive radio ranging measures distance between tanker and receiver. Except for mandatory calls to flight centres, little conversation is heard. (For many years the radio call designator 'Aspen' was used to identify the SR-71 to traffic controllers.)

A Tacan transmitter on the tanker provides the SR-71 crew with range and bearing data for a head-on rendezvous. At 22–24 miles (41–44 km) range the tanker begins a 180° turn onto the same heading as the SR-71, allowing the latter to fall in trail and gradually catch up, covering the last 3–4 miles (5–7 km) decelerating to equal speed. About one mile from the tanker the SR-71 is in the pre-contact (usually visual) position and begins to edge closer. The tanker boom operator signals all is ready by nodding the refuelling boom up and down. As the SR-71 looms closer, he might call out the distance-to-go. '100 feet . . . 50 . . . 30 . . . 20 . . . 10 . . . contact!'

The tanker copilot can now activate the fuel transfer valves and booster pumps, delivering JP-7 fuel to the SR-71 at some 5,500 lb/min. The refuelling boom also provides a private communication link between the SR-71 and the tanker while in contact, so instructions or messages can be passed (usually terse and business like, but occasionally enlivened with humour) as both crewmen work to achieve the most rapid and efficient transfer of roughly 70,000 lb (31,818 kg) or so of fuel.

SR-71A 64-17969 was lost in the early seventies after crashing in Thailand (via Chris Pocock)

SR-71A 64-17961 shortly after topping up with JP-7 (Lockheed-California)

KC-135Q serial 59-0117, high-speed boom extended, seen from the stabilized pre-contact position of a receiver. In 1981, this aircraft was operated by the 100th ARW and based at Beale
(Paul F Crickmore)

Tanker rendezvous is typically conducted at 350 knots (648 km/h or Mach 0.81) at 26,000 ft (7929 m). This altitude is lower than SR-71 crews would prefer, but it is about as high as a fully laden KC-135 can operate while maintaining 350 knots indicated airspeed. It would be undesirable to attempt refuelling at a much lower speed because the SR-71 is very heavy towards the end of the refuelling operation; at lower speeds it would attain a higher angle of attack, inducing additional aerodynamic drag. Refuelling has occurred at 31,000 ft (9451 m) but the two flight envelopes are less compatible. Future operations with KC-10 tankers will allow refuelling up to 33,000 ft (10,061 m) and Mach 0.88, which will provide a comfortable safety factor.

Some 12–13 minutes after first contact, the SR-71 unplugs from the tanker. On some routine training missions from Beale this usually is achieved near Boise, Idaho. The SR-71 pilot reduces power slightly, drops back from the tanker and slips out to the right. When clear, full afterburner power is applied and the SR-71 passes the tanker rapidly, climbing out of sight.

Tracking about 070° the aircraft passes over the mountain wilderness of the northwest USA. A 10° angle of attack (AOA) is initially maintained and speed is allowed to reach Mach 0.9. North of Yellowstone National Park the aircraft reaches 30,000 ft (9146 m); the nose angle is lowered slightly and speed builds up to Mach 0.95. About 30 seconds later the aircraft is passing 33,000 ft (10,061 m) and longitudinal trim checks are completed before entering the supersonic flight regime.

A minimum energy Rutowski climb technique is used to minimize the effects of transonic drag. This descent/climb 'dipsy doodle' manoeuvre is normally employed and involves descending to approximately 29,000 ft (8841 m) (or even lower when the ambient temperature is higher); at a rate of descent of around 2,500 ft/min, a constant 450 knots (833 km/h) indicated airspeed is maintained as the aircraft slips through Mach 1. As Mach 1.25 is achieved the climb is renewed and momentarily the engine control system unlocks the engine inlet spike for optimum pressure recovery; the pilot does not intervene and concentrates on nailing the speed buildup. An

autopilot mode can even take on this acceleration chore if the pilot selects the automatic climb mode. The usual technique is to hold 450 knots (833 km/h) indicated until Mach 2.7, then allow the indicated airspeed to fall in 10 knot (18.5 km/h) increments as the climb progresses, but aiming to reach Mach 3.0 at 75,000 ft (22,866 m) and level off. Cruise climb to above 80,000 ft (24,390 m) can be achieved by reducing the indicated airspeed as fuel is burned off. Throughout the climb and cruise the pilot monitors optimum performance using a digital instrument called the Triple Display Indicator, which displays Mach number, altitude, and knots equivalent airspeed (KEAS).

Training missions head eastwards towards the top of the climb, and from somewhere over southeast Montana, a right banked turn is usually commenced onto a southerly track, taking the aircraft somewhere east of Denver. On a mission of this sort the crew will be monitoring available diversion airbases, and the criteria is usually that they should be in a wedge about 45° across, and about 200 miles (370 km) ahead of the aircraft. An SR-71 cannot lose altitude and speed rapidly enough to reach a base directly below without a great teardrop turn to reduce forward momentum. Over the northern parts of New Mexico the aircraft is banked to the west, and after passing over southern Arizona and Nevada, near to Las Vegas, a turn to the

SR-71A 64-17967 being refuelled near Boise, Idaho (Paul F Crickmore Collection)

OVERLEAF
SR-71A '955 during refuelling tests with the Boeing 747 prototype; no fuel was transferred but the test confirmed that there was no unfavourable aerodynamic interaction between the two aircraft. Boeing were unsuccessful in their bid to capture a US Air Force order for a 747 tanker/cargo aircraft (Lockheed-California)

right takes the aircraft up California, where top of descent commences near Yosemite National Park.

Afterburner power is reduced at first, then cancelled completely, leaving the aircraft in a long decelerating descent, but still with full non-afterburner power selected on both engines. As in all modes of high Mach flying, there is little margin for complacency at the pre-descent point. Engine and airframe performance limitations impose boundaries on the permissible speed and altitude combinations that are acceptable, leaving the crew with no

A fine example of swirling vortices, generated by an SR-71 in landing configuration (Sgt G L Jones)

alternative but to keep the major flight parameters under continuous and careful scrutiny. The compressor airflow cools rapidly, and a constant 350 knots (648 km/h) equivalent airspeed is recommended to minimize inlet disturbances. Throttle and autopilot scheduling can be used to fly the descent profile, maintaining a high proportion of laminar flow throughout the engine system, and avoiding the chance of temperature runaways during engine compressor stalls or 'unstarts'. There is little latitude for variations from the pre-determined profile until the speed has slowed to Mach 1.3 around 30,000 ft (9146 m). The aircraft will normally be at approximately Mach 2.5 at 70,000 ft (21,341 m), Mach 2 at 60,000 ft (18,293 m) and Mach 1.6 at 45,000 ft (13,719

m). The descent from 70,000 ft to 35,000 ft takes about 10 minutes.

Below 30,000 ft (9146 m) the aircraft is again flying at subsonic speeds, and would be in a position either to begin the final descent phase into Beale or to rendezvous with a tanker again, in which case it would fly another high-speed loop around the Western US.

Returning to land the crew concentrate briefly on transferring 4,000 lb (1818 kg) of fuel forward, thus bringing the aircraft's centre of gravity forward, thereby trimming out the forward translation of the centre of pressure, so restoring the aircraft to a subsonic aerodynamic configuration, necessary for low speed manoeuvring. (The aerodynamic centre of pressure moves forward about 9 per cent of the mean aerodynamic chord in the transonic transition).

The landing circuit is entered at 1,700 ft (518 m) above the ground and at 300 knots (555 km/h) indicated airspeed for a 360° overhead fighter-style approach. Beale approach control will have been monitoring the returning aircraft and as it reaches the close vicinity control is passed to the tower controller who can authorize a visual approach 'run and break'

SR-71A 64-17962 with brake parachute deployed (Lockheed-California)

down the active runway. This is common practise at the end of an SR-71 sortie, with the break culminating in a 60° banked turn that is allowed to unwind gradually as 180° of turn is completed and an opposite direction 'downwind' position is reached. Speed will have reduced to 250 knots (463 km/h) in the manoeuvre, and the gear is extended. The aircraft has a noticeable nose-up attitude at these relatively low speeds, and would be about 8° up from the horizontal in level flight by the time that gear was extended.

On base leg turn another 20 knots (37 km/h) of speed is lost, and then on final approach the speed is further reduced to 175 knots, (324 km/h) by which time the aircraft is flying at about 10° nose-up. The flare brings further increases in the upward body deck angle, and a final reduction in speed to about 155 knots (287 km/h) at touchdown. Pilots report good visibility even during the nose-high approach angle and they are assisted in the stable flare by a strong ground effect; the delta wing airflow cushions the touchdown for smooth 'oiler' landings. Engine power is reduced immediately on touchdown and the braking parachute is deployed. Deceleration hits 1G

momentarily as the big bite of the orange 'chute slows the aircraft rapidly below 100 knots (185 km/h). At 55 knots (102 km/h) the parachute is jettisoned, still fully inflated to ensure clean separation and prevent the heavy shroud-line clevis from damaging the fuselage skin. Total landing distance from a typical sortie is about 4,000 ft (1219 m).

Although the flight portion is now completed, all is not yet finished. After clearing the runway, the RSO begins to read through the after-landing checks. On return to the shelter, pre-shutdown checks are completed and the engines stopped. The wheels are chocked and fans are placed adjacent to the main gear on both sides to cool the brakes; taxying at lightweight with high residual thrust at idle engine

SR-71B 64-17957 receives a final dousing from a fire crew after crashing within seven miles of Beale on 11 January 1968. Instructor pilot Lt Col Robert G Sowers and his student, Capt David E Fruehauf, ejected safely (Appeal-Democrat)

power makes them very hot. The canopies rise and the crewmen open their face plates before the steps are drawn alongside so they can be assisted in disconnecting their life support equipment. With ejection seat safety pins inserted, helmets off, and fresh warm Californian air entering their lungs again the two men settle into the recliner armchairs of the van that takes them back to the PSD buildings.

Once in the building the men shed their pressure suits, jump in the shower, and change into their orange flight suits for a detailed maintenance debrief on the aircraft's flight performance. Meanwhile, magnetic tapes have already been removed from the aircraft and processed for fine-parameter analysis. The maintenance crew review the aircraft's onboard data recorder where information is gathered at five second intervals throughout the flight; this instrument yields valuable data about the state of the aircraft's systems which is transferred to a databank. The cameras, each on their individual pallets, are lowered onto custom-built trolleys and taken to the 9th Reconnaissance Technical Squadron to be checked for performance.

Training and testing

Together with crew training the 9th SRW were also responsible for phase 3 operational testing. Intense trials activity with a new aircraft inevitably leads to accidents. The first to be suffered by the unit occurred at 20:23 hr on 13 April 1967. After tanking, crew E-12 began climbing SR-71A serial 64-17966 to altitude. Over-extending the angle of attack (AOA), the nose was eased down slightly to regain airspeed. A second pull-up also proved too hard, and after an accelerated pitch-up the aircraft departed from controlled flight. Both men ejected from a deep stall but escaped unhurt. The aircraft tumbled out of the sky and crashed near Las Vegas in New Mexico.

Six months later on the evening of 25 October 1967, a dining in night was being held at the Beale Officer's Club with 'Mr Skunk Works' himself, Kelly Johnson, as guest of honour. High above, crew E-18 began descending SR-71 serial 64-17965 on autopilot

The foam covered carcass of SR-71A 64-17977 after an unsuccessful runway abort on 10 October 1968. Despite the efforts of Maj Gabriel A Kardong and RSO Maj James A Kogler, the aircraft was a write-off (Appeal-Democrat)

over central Nevada; there was no visible horizon and scattered ground lights merged with the stars. Unknown to the crew, the INS gyro platform had tumbled (no warning lights were fitted to alert them). The aircraft entered a steep descent and dropped a wing. With much of the flight instrumentation depending upon the failed gyro platform for attitude information, the first sign the crew had was a steady speed increase. In total darkness, in a steep dive and no external visual reference available the crew had little alternative. The RSO ejected at about Mach 1.4 and the pilot followed him shortly afterwards. Both men escaped unhurt and the aircraft crashed near Lovelock, Nevada, at 20:30 hours.

Yet another accident befell the 9th SRW about three months later on Thursday, 11 January 1968. One of their most experienced instructor pilots (the commander of the 99th SRS) was airborne from Beale in SR-71B 64-17957 with a student on his third training flight. They were turning for home over northern Washington state when the aircraft suffered a double generator failure. Immediately switching off all non-essential electrics, they were forced to rely on 30 minutes of battery power. A decision was made to press on for home when it was discovered that Portland, Oregon, was overcast and snowed out. With gravity now supplying fuel to the engines instead of the electrically operated fuel pumps, the two pilots skillfully coaxed the Blackbird back to Beale. Slowing down on a long straight-in final at 3,000 ft (915 m) disaster struck. The natural nose-up angle of attack of 10° allowed some of the fuel inlet ports to 'suck air' from already empty tanks and interrupted the fuel flow to the engine combustion chambers causing cavitation and a double flame-out. At traffic pattern altitude, after repeated airstarts and flame-outs, both men ejected safely. The aircraft stalled and pancaked inverted into the ground about seven miles (12 km) north of the field.

On 29 July 1968 an experienced crew saved an aircraft despite serious engine problems. Accelerating through Mach 2.88 and 68,000 ft (20,732 m) a violent explosion occurred in the right engine. The fire warning light illuminated and the pilot immediately referred to the engine fire check list. The

Maj James W Hudson was killed after an unsuccessful ejection attempt from this T-38 during a takeoff accident at Beale on 23 March 1971. Instructor pilot Lt Col Jack R Thornton elected to stay with the aircraft and sustained minor back injuries
(*Appeal-Democrat)*

fire warning light remained on and, using the internal rear-view mirrors and periscope, a fire was visually confirmed. Despite the danger of an explosion the crew elected to remain with the aircraft and attempt an emergency landing. After throwing the fuel cut off switch to the sick engine the fire warning light went out for a few seconds—only to come back on again for the rest of the flight. Despite the loss of the right engine and severe flight control difficulties due to airframe fire damage, the crew managed to land the aircraft safely.

A newly trained crew was less fortunate with factory-fresh 64-17977. As they began their takeoff run down runway 14 at Beale on 10 October 1968, a wheel failure blasted shrapnel through the fuel cells in the aircraft's belly, starting a spectacular fire. During the takeoff abort, the remaining tyres on the gear truck also blew. The fire consumed the brake 'chute and as the aircraft crossed the far end of the runway it cut clean through the barrier cable. The RSO ejected successfully, but the pilot decided to stay for the violent high-speed sledge ride across nearly half-a-mile of rough overrun, emerging with sprains and bruises. Meanwhile, as the RSO descended by parachute he noticed that the aircraft had started a grass fire directly underneath him, but he managed to avoid a roasting. Number 17977 was written off.

At 09:15 on Wednesday 17 June 1970, crew E-08 disconnected '970 from the tanker facing the morning sun. The pilot momentarily lost sight of the KC-135. He collided sharply with its horizontal stabilizer, completely severing the nose from the SR-71. With the now non-aerodynamic airframe completely unflyable both he and the RSO were forced to eject. They landed safely 20 miles (37 km) east of El Paso as the SR-71 smashed into the ground nearby.

The tanker crew carried out a controlability check and, finding that all functioned well, pin-pointed the SR-71 and flew carefully back to Beale. Upon recovery, the crew found that the stabilizer had virtually parted company from the rest of the aircraft—they had been fortunate to retain control.

The first fatal accident involving the 9th SRW at Beale happened on Tuesday 23 March 1971 when T-38 0-91606 failed to get airborne on a routine 75-minute training sortie. Takeoff was aborted at lift off because of serious flight control difficulties but the pilot in the rear cockpit was killed when he ejected too

SR-71A 64-17958, complete with a large white cross to aid ground tracking and calibration, crewed by Capt Eldon W 'Al' Joersz and RSO Maj 'GT' Morgan for the world speed record runs on 27/28 July 1976. Their 2,193.167 mph (3529.56 km/h) over a 15/26 km course still stands with the other SR-71 records (Lockheed-California)

near the ground and his 'chute failed to deploy in time. The front seater stayed with the aircraft and managed to bring it to a halt near the end of the runway. He received minor back injuries. Pitch control was lost because the elevator push rod had become disconnected. It resulted in the only known fatality of an SR-71 pilot.

An evaluation undertaken by SR-71s of the 9th SRW in the early seventies entitled 'Eagle Bait' was designed to determine the interceptibility of a high-speed, high-altitude target by an F-15 Eagle. As the SR-71 tracked swiftly up California, F-15s accelerated at FL400 and pulled into zoom climbs to try and formate with the faster target plane.

A large percentage of California's population were subjected to sonic booms and the effort was terminated early. It was reinstated later—this time over the Pacific—but when the programme ended it was found that the F-15 was generally ineffective against such a fast, high target. This effort allowed a reasonable appraisal of the potential outcome of MiG-25 intercepts.

On 1 April 1971 the 99th SRS was deactivated as an SR-71 unit and reactivated as a U-2 squadron elsewhere. Drastic as such action might appear, it was in fact a paper transfer of aircrew members to the 1st SRS. Originally perceived as two 20 crew squadrons, such growth proved unnecessary and prohibitively expensive.

Finally, in the 1970s, certain aircrews enjoyed brief periods of high public profile setting a series of official world records. The recognition events began on 26 April 1971, when an SR-71A flown by Lt Col Thomas B Estes and his RSO Lt Col Dewain C Vick flew 15,000 miles (27,777 km) non-stop (the equivalent of flying from San Francisco to Paris and back), more than half way around the world in 10 hours 30 minutes. For this achievement the crew were awarded the 1971 Mackay Trophy for, 'The most meritorious flight of the year', and the 1972 Harmon International Trophy for, 'The most outstanding international achievement in the art/science of aeronautics'.

On 27/28 July 1976, as part of the bicentennial celebrations, the 9th SRW conducted a series of record flights in the vicinity of Edwards AFB, which resulted in six new world speed and altitude records verified and authenticated by the *Federation Aeronautique Internationale* (FAI).

Speed Over A Closed Course (a 1000 km course).

Maj Adolphus H Bledsoe Jr pilot and Maj John T Fuller, RSO, flew an SR-71A at 2,092.294 mph (3367.221 km/h). This flight brought the record back to the USA, having been lost to the E-266, an experimental version of the MiG-25. Each record set also automatically qualified the aeroplane for the 'Class C-1 Group 111 (Jet) Without Payload' category.

Altitude In Horizontal Flight

Capt Robert C Helt, pilot and Maj Larry A Elliott, RSO, flew an SR-71A to 85,068.997 ft (25,929.031 m). Taking the record away from the YF-12A. (This same crew had flown this mission the previous day, a few feet lower. It was reflown because weather interfered with the photographic verification required for certification).

Speed Over A Closed Course (15/25 km straight course).

Capt Eldon W Joersz, pilot and Maj George T Morgan, Jr, RSO took SR-71A to a speed of 2193.167 mph (3529.56 km/h). (Again this record was previously held by a YF-12A. FAI certification requires the aircraft to accomplish two consecutive passes, without varying its altitude more than 150 ft

Photographed on 28 July 1976 are (left to right): Col John Storrie (9th SRW commander), Maj 'GT' Morgan, Paul Mellinger (the Lockheed representative at Beale), and Capt Eldon 'Al' Joersz (via Paul F Crickmore)

(46 m) between each pass. As with Helt and Elliott this record attempt was also made the previous day, but was re-run because of incomplete verification).

Altitude accuracy is provided for the FAI on the ground by two methods. One is by radar, which is accurate to within 170 ft (52 m); and the other by highly calibrated cameras. On Joersz's second pass the day before, high cloud prevented photo verification during the last few seconds of the run.

In a highly publicized flight on 1 September 1974, the 9th SRW claimed yet another Class C-1, Group 111 (Jet) record.

Speed Over A Recognized Course—New York to London

Code-named 'Exercise Glowing Speed', the pilot was Maj James Sullivan, with RSO Maj Noel Widdifield. To ensure that no last minute problems would mar a

TOP LEFT
Maj John Fuller (left) and pilot Maj Adolphus H Bledsoe receive media attention after their successful speed record bid on 28 July 1976. They achieved 2,092.294 mph (3367.221 km/h) around a 1000 km course

BOTTOM LEFT
Left to right: Maj Bill Flannigan (RSO), Maj 'GT' Morgan (RSO), Lt Col Cal Jewett (pilot), and Lt Col Bob Helt (pilot) pose in their David Clark Company S1030 'gold suits', now standard issue for SR-71 crews. As a captain on 28 July 1976, Helt flew 64/17962 to a new altitude record of 85,068.997 ft (25,929.031 m)

ABOVE
Maj James Sullivan and RSO Maj Noel Widdifield touch down at Farnborough in 64-17972 after establishing a new speed record between New York and London

OVERLEAF (inset)
In white experimental S901J pressure suits, Sullivan (left) and Widdenfield are congratulated by Republican Senator F Edward Herbert at Farnborough (Lockheed-California)

OVERLEAF
A recent photograph of the transatlantic record breaker: SR-71 64-17972 lands back at Mildenhall after an operational flight. '972 sports the current paint scheme, which is devoid of all national markings, and a small red serial number on each fin. According to the Hague Convention on 1907, a military aircraft must bear conspicuously placed insignia (Paul F Crickmore)

high-visibility effort, a backup aircraft and crew were ready. Lifting off from Beale in SR-71A, 17972, Sullivan completed his first air refuelling shortly afterwards on the Reno to Boise refuelling track and headed for the eastern seaboard. After completing the second refuelling '972 climbed to altitude and cruising speed before knifing through the high altitude time gate over New York city. Cruising on a direct track for the London time gate a descent and second subsonic refuelling and climb back to cruise altitude was accomplised well to the north of the Azores.

At the London Air Traffic Control Centre at RAF West Drayton, excitement grew as the first high-speed trace was observed on the Cossor SSR 700 radar, 'piped' in from the site at Burrington. At 30° West, the aircraft was running eight minutes early. As it entered the UK Upper Information Region (UIR), the 'afterglow' on the radar screen gave it the appearance of a miniature comet, while other airline aircraft far below in its area seemed to remain stationary in comparison. Clearing the London time gate, Sullivan decelerated and descended for another lightweight refuelling over the North Sea from a tanker flying from RAF Mildenhall in Suffolk. Sullivan then proceeded to the Royal Aircraft Establishment Farnborough for landing where '972 was the top attraction at the airshow. They had crossed the North Atlantic (a distance of some 3,490 miles), in 1 hour 54 min 56.4 sec, averaging 1,806.964 mph).

On landing President Gerald Ford spoke by telephone with Sullivan and Widdifield. He told them it was . . . 'a great flight and a magnificent accomplishment for the United States and the Air Force'.

Having stolen the show at Farnborough and capturing the imagination of millions around the world, there was yet more to follow. After several days of public display, '972 was flown to RAF Mildenhall and readied for the trip home to Beale.

On 12 September Capt Harold B Adams and his RSO Maj William C Machorek, were to set another world speed record, this time between London and Los Angeles. It was not to be that day—only ten minutes after passing through the London time gate, oil pressure fluctuations indicated a problem in one of the engines. Adams aborted the attempt and recovered the aircraft back to Mildenhall. Moisture had accumulated around the oil pressure gauge sensor, causing the instrument to give a false reading.

But the next day proved luckier for both crew members and assured their place in the record books—they streaked back to LA at an average speed of 1,435.587 mph. The first refuelling was conducted over SW Scotland before passing back through the London gate, while a second refuelling was accomplished over the Atlantic and a third over Canada; yet another lightweight refuelling took place after passing through the LA gate on the way back to Beale.

The 5,645 miles (10,454 km) between gates was flown in 3 hr 47 min 35.8 sec. The LA Press carped about a sonic boom on the descent. A minor compressor stall was encountered and cured by temporary increase in the power settings, but it caused the transition to subsonic flight to be further west than planned resulting in the shock wake being spread on the eastern part of the LA basin.

The Middle East (1973–74)

Frustrated by the boundary positions at the conclusion of the 1967 Six Day War and anxious to advance the political process in his country, President Sadat of Egypt decided that war with Israel was necessary to re-establish claims on former Egyptian lands beyond the Suez Canal. He gained agreement from President Assad of Syria to mount a simultaneous attack on Israel from the north. At 14:00 on Saturday 6 October 1973 (the Jewish Day of Atonement—Yom Kippur Day) a war began that caught most intelligence agencies of the West off guard. The Soviets launched Cosmos 596 three days earlier from Plesetsk in the south western USSR. It was equipped with low-resolution cameras to conduct regular surveillance of the battle area.

The Egyptians opened up a barrage from 2,000 guns which lasted for 53 minutes along the entire front. Simultaneously, 240 Egyptian aircraft hit three Israeli airfields in the Sinai and other important targets. Within 15 minutes the Egyptians were advancing along a 130 mile (240 km) front with five infantry divisions supported by three mechanized and two armoured divisions. That land force rumbled over ten bridges that had been thrown across the Suez Canal and established foot-holds on the east bank. At the same moment, the Syrian phase of the attack was opened in the north with another massive artillery bombardment which lasted 50 minutes. This heavy barrage presaged the advance of three Syrian Infantry divisions, and two armoured divisions. Simultaneously, an independent attack was mounted by Syrian helicopter-borne troops on the important Israeli observation post at Mount Hermon.

As the Israelis attacked Egyptian bridgeheads on 8 October, and the Syrians got closer to the River Jordan and the Sea of Galilee, the Soviets launched another reconnaissance satellite, Cosmos 597. Later identified as a 'close-look vehicle', Cosmos 597 had the interesting capability of changing its orbit by firing manoeuvring rockets to lower its apogee for improved photographic resolution. Its path was inclined 65.4° to the Equator, which aligned it perfectly to carry it up and across both fronts.

As Cosmos 596 was recovered on the 9th, the situation on the ground turned in favour of the Israelis. In the north the Syrian effort had been fought to a standstill after a furious battle. To the south General Sheron's forces attacked the Egyptians

Capt Ty Judkins (left) and Capt 'GT' Morgan (crew E-08), prepare to sip a well earned glass of champagne after their nonstop mission over the Middle East in 1973. Both men are wearing chocolate brown S901J pressure suits

to retake a second-line fortification that had fallen the day before.

On 10 October the Soviets launched Cosmos 598 to continue surveillance of the war zone. Pitched slightly higher than earlier 'birds' of the Cosmos series, 598 was in orbit the next day as 597 returned its film cassettes to Earth. With the possibility of the Soviets receiving real-time imagery from 598 via the Yevpatoriya tracking station in the Crimea, the United States also required quality intelligence.

Under conditions of utmost secrecy, fuel and support equipment moved to Griffiss AFB in New York to support a short-term SR-71 operation to monitor the war from the eastern seaboard of the United States. The SR-71 'Giant Scale' concept of global reconnaissance was about to undergo its most demanding operational test.

On 12 October 1973 a single SR-71 left Griffiss. Flying on a direct track for Gibraltar, the pilot locked the aircraft's autopilot into a Mach 3 cruise-hold shortly after post-takeoff refuelling from a KC-135Q. Cruising steadily at high Mach for over an hour, afterburners were cut off for a normal 20 minute descent profile to level flight at FL260 for a second aerial refuelling. Off the Azores, the aircraft gulped another load of fuel from European-based tankers, as scheduled. Fifteen minutes later, there followed another cruise climb to 80,000 ft (24,390 m) and Mach 3.0. Another descent for aerial refuelling commenced west of Crete. Close to a threat zone, it was considered prudent to provide a combat air patrol (CAP) during refuelling of US Navy F-4s from carriers operating in the Mediterranean.

Completing this refuelling, the tankers returned to their base while the SR-71 again accelerated to top

SR-71A 64-17968 on public display at Malmstron AFB in August 1975. The silver-walled tyres are impregnated with aluminium powder to reflect the heat generated by high-speed cruising flight away from the gear bay and tyres (Dick Gerdes via Robert F Dorr)

Mach and altitude. Operating in the eastern Mediterranean, the SR-71 was able to collect data from the southern and northern fronts that would prove invaluable in peace negotiations.

Clearing Egyptian airspace, the SR-71 again decelerated and descended to refuel before leaving the Mediterranean area.

The flight back was a reversal of the earlier transatlantic flight with tankers, including ground alert spares, at Griffiss, should the weather be unsuitable for landing in the northern US. The weather was perfect however, and at 10 am on the morning of 13 October the SR-71 landed back at Griffiss after just over ten hours of flight, having covered more than 11,000 miles (20,370 km)—a new milestone in operational performance.

The next day an official Egyptian military communiqué announced that 'two reconnaissance planes, of a type only possessed by the United States, flew over Egypt yesterday for a period of 25 minutes'. Identifying the aircraft as SR-71s, it continued 'the two reconnaissance planes violated Egyptian airspace at 11:03 GMT over Port Said, went deep into Egypt at Nagaa Hammady 366 miles (590 km), south of Cairo, turned back over the capital and flew eastward in the direction of Jordan and Syria, then turned back to the Mediterranean. Flying at an altitude of 25 km (about 15 miles) the two planes made the round trip in 25 minutes'. The communiqué ended 'this was the first time that Egypt's airspace has been violated by this type of plane'.

The track described in the communqué is most likely accurate; what makes it interesting is the apparent mistake made by the Egyptians in incorrectly identifying the number of aircraft involved. This discrepancy might be attributable to the difficulty in tracking such a high performance target with a small radar cross section. On the other hand, it could have been a deliberate ploy to exaggerate the claim or to mask their true radar capabilities. Other possibilities might be that the double sonic boom deceived ground witnesses, or the aircraft was jamming.

On the 14th, the military situation facing the Syrians in the north was becoming increasingly desperate. The Soviets had stepped up their airlift aware that the entire Syrian front was now in danger of collapse. The Soviet Ambassador to the United States, Anatoly Dobrynin, said Soviet airborne forces were now on full alert and ready to move to the defence of Damascus. Israeli forces had encircled the Egyptian Third Army on the East Bank of the Jordan River by the 21st, and the Egyptian military situation was becoming more acute by the day and hour. Fighting eventually stopped on 24 October.

As Cosmos 602 was blasted into orbit on 20 October Cosmos 600 (launched on 14 October) was being readied for recovery on the 23rd. The Soviets had maintained constant satellite surveillance over the war zone throughout the conflict. They were thus able to provide a stream of grim intelligence to their decision makers. SR-71 operations against the same area numbered approximately ten. The first two were flown from Griffiss. When the first snows of winter arrived the operation 'migrated' to Seymour Johnson AFB in North Carolina. Security was maintained throughout these operations. Fighter, bomber and tanker crew members at the host bases were briefed by security officers, to mention nothing of the black aircraft undergoing 'test flights' over the Atlantic. Operations conducted employing strict radio silence insured a significant level of surprise during most missions. A high degree of mission success was enjoyed by all crews, flying each mission 'as prescribed'. These ten hour duration flights, consisted of five air refuellings, and five hours of Mach 3 time. They continued into January 1974 and provide independent photographic evidence at the negotiation table to the deeply distrusting Egyptians and Israelis, during very delicate withdrawl operations. The SR thus vindicated the concept of global reconnaissance and provided 'hot-spot analysis' and 'time-frame flexibility', not enjoyed by satellites. Additionally, these missions proved that manned reconnaissance aircraft could still operate successfully on short notice in areas possessing a sophisticated air defence system.

On 1 August 1981, the 4029 Strategic Reconnaissance Training Squadron was formed at Beale AFB. As a component squadron of the 9th SRW, its task was originally to train U-2 pilots. This training operation was soon extended to encompass both U-2/TR-1 and SR-71 operations, and now trains these reconnaissance crew members to full 'combat ready' status.

Giant Plate

Cuba occasionally attracts the interest of her northern neighbour's reconnaissance gathering platforms. Part of the need for surveillance can be attributed to that country's continued programme of testing the resolve of the United States to deal with varying degrees of provocation perpetrated by Castro and his Soviet allies.

The SR-71 still represents a key asset in the United States wide ranging reconnaissance systems that observe Cuba. Flown from Beale AFB under the mission code named 'Giant Plate', many SR-71 sorties are of a stand-off nature and are flown

exclusively in international airspace. A typical training profile might call for the first air refuelling to take place shortly after take-off from Beale. Following a cruise climb to high speed and altitude across the United States, a let down would be initiated, to make good a second air refuelling somewhere along the eastern seaboard. Having accomplished a second cruise climb back to high Mach and altitude over the Atlantic, the airplane could then turn to fly nearby the islands and directly back to Beale AFB. This return route takes the SR-71 over the Gulf of Mexico, Texas, New Mexico, Arizona and Nevada before recovering back at Beale. The round trip would last between $3\frac{1}{2}$ and 4 hours.

Occasionally, and on specific instructions from high authority, this track can be modified to carry the aircraft directly over Cuba. In an act of goodwill towards Cuba, the incoming Carter administration suspended manned reconnaissance flights against the islands. In January 1978, however, a US reconnaissance satellite detected a Soviet freighter unloading a number of crates at Havana. Intelligence specialists believed that the crates contained MiG-23s. Later in the year, the crates were removed from the dockside to a nearby airbase, where the aircraft were reassembled. The 'crateologists' were correct: in all, fifteen new MiG-23s had been supplied to Castro. Some Administration Officials in the US saw such an upgrading of Cuban air strength as 'worrying'. It was known that the Soviets had been supplying two versions of the MiG-23 to their allies. One, the MiG-23E, was an interceptor; the other, called the MiG-23F or MiG-27, was a ground attack aircraft capable of delivering nuclear weapons. It was the latter variant that caused consternation on Capitol Hill. By supplying the 'attack' type to Castro, Moscow was violating a 1962 pledge of not deploying 'offensive' weapons to Cuba.

On 16 November 1978 it was decided that an SR-71 should be flown over Cuba in order to identify the variant. Two flights are believed to have taken place in parallel with political moves. President Carter had said on 20 November that the Soviet Union had assured him, publically and privately, that the MiG-23 jets were in Cuba for defensive purposes only. A *Pravda* newspaper commentary (carried in advance of publication by the Tass newsagency) cited American Press reports that 'the presence of such aircraft would run counter to the 1962 agreement' were 'groundless and provokatory from beginning to end'.

Photographic reconnaissance secured by the SR-71 was able to confirm Soviet claims.

In August 1979 a US intelligence satellite provided imagery of a large Soviet troop presence on the Island. On Friday, 28 September 1979 or Saturday, 29 September 1979, an SR-71 flew over the island to determine the size and strength of the unit. It revealed that some 3,000 men with 40 tanks and other equipment were indeed stationed southwest of

DECANO DEL PERIODISMO NACIONAL

Director
Don Pablo Antonio Cuadra
Co-Director
Lic. Pedro J. Chamorro B.
Gerente General
Ing. Jaime Chamorro C.

El Diario de los
nicaragüenses.   Fundado el 2 de Marzo de 1926

APARTADO No. 192

AL SERVICIO DE LA VERDAD Y LA JUSTICIA
Managua, Viernes 9 de Noviembre de 1984   TELEX 375-2051

Sin Libertad de Prensa no hay Libertad

 C$ 5.00

12 PAGINAS
EDICION No. 17,171

LA PRENSA

Washington todavía dudoso

Moscú asegura: no son Migs

WASHINGTON, NOV. (EFE).- La Unión Soviética ha informado a Estados Unidos de que no ha enviado cazas de combate a Nicaragua, dijo hoy el secretario de Estado, George Shultz.

Al parecer, los desmentidos de Moscú y de Managua sobre el envío de los "Mig 21" no han convencido aún a la administración Reagan que el problema esté resuelto, señala el diario.

El secretario de Estado precisó, sin embargo, que no tenía conocimiento de planes estadounidenses para invadir Nicaragua.

(En Managua, el gobierno sandinista ha anunciado una movilización de estudiantes para prepararse ante una posible invasión de Estados Unidos.)

El canciller nicaragüense Miguel D'Escoto negó el miércoles que aviones soviéticos de combate estuvieran camino de su país.

Pasa a la Pág. 12 No. 1

La agencia UPI transmitió hoy esta foto del SR-71, el avión de reconocimiento de alto vuelo, conocido como "Pájaro Negro" que causó los estampidos que se oyeron el jueves y el viernes en Managua y otras ciudades del país. La capitana Rosa Pasos, vocera del Ministerio de Defensa, afirmó que el avión ha sido plenamente identificado como el "SR-71", dijo la agencia noticiosa. (Radiofoto UPI)

Convocado el Consejo de Seguridad ONU

MANAGUA, NOV. 9. (ACAN-EFE).- El canciller nicaragüense, Miguel D'Escoto, declaró ayer que Nicaragua está viviendo una situación "extremadamente grave" ante la posibilidad de que Estados Unidos realice acciones militares directas contra este país.

"Nadie desconoce la obsesión de la Administración Reagan por aplastar la Revolución Popular Sandinista", dijo D'Escoto en rueda de prensa, al anunciar la convocatoria del Consejo de Seguridad de las Naciones Unidas para analizar estos hechos.

D'Escoto manifestó que Estados Unidos está desempeñando una política hacia Nicaragua como la de cualquier "bandolero internacional".

La convocatoria del Consejo

Pasa a la Pág. 12 No. 2

Estruendo escuchado hoy a las 8:30 am.

Nuevo vuelo del "Pájaro Negro"

MANAGUA, NOV. 9.- Una nueva explosión aérea se escuchó hoy aquí, presumiblemente causada por un avión espía suspersónico que sobrevuela el espacio aéreo nicaragüen-

las 8:30 horas (14:30 GMT) y fue escuchada por los habitantes de la capital, que se mostraron alarmados.

Estruendos similares se escucharon ayer, a la misma hora en diversos sectores del

denunció que las "explosiones" de ayer fueron ocasionadas por un avión norteamericano del tipo "SR-71".

La cancillería de Managua ha cursado notas de protesta

Unidos por el espionaje supersónico "que sólo se lanza en casos de una crisis en evolución grave".

MANAGUA, NOV. 9. (UPI).- Nicaragua afirmó hoy que un avión espía de

na del país por segundo día consecutivo, añadiendo que ello es el preludio de una invasión contra la nación centroamericana.

El gobierno sandinista movilizó a unos 20,000 estudian-

transmitía hoy continuos mensajes a la población pidiendo que esté pendiente para recibir informaciones importantes.

El avión, no identificado independientemente, pasó

Nuevas maniobras

Havana. This new information caused considerable concern in US Government circles threatening blockage of the US Senates' ratification of the Strategic Arms Limitation Treaty then pending with the Soviet Union. In a TV address to the nation President Carter said that there was no immediate threat to the US, and that the Soviets claimed that the troops positions were only a training centre, which would not be enlarged. The President went on to state that he would take steps to monitor activities in the area. The SR-71 flight a few days later was a vital element in those continuing surveillance plans.

During Solid Shield 83, a force of some 47,000 US servicemen took part in manoeuvres in the vicintiy of Cuba and Central America. Supported by several warships and an undisclosed number of aircraft, the annual exercise was brought forward from May to the second half of April. Perhaps not unconnected with this exercise was the fact that another SR-71 entered Cuban airspace and allegedly flew back and forth from west to east between 10:05 and 11:00 on Tuesday, 26 April 1983. This somewhat blatant piece of 'sonic sabre rattling' occurred on the 22nd Anniversary of the Playa Giron invasion, perhaps better known as the Bay of Pigs incident.

The SR-71 hits the headlines in Nicaragua after its sonic booms were heard in the capital, Managua

As new crews entered the programme, the thorough training that each underwent often paid dividends during major upsets in the cockpit, as a crew discovered during the recovery phase of an operational mission. After a sharp series of engine inlet malfunctions the right engine compressor stalled. The pilot decided to shutdown the troublesome right engine and make an emergency single-engined approach. Descending to radar pattern altitude, the left engine oil pressure started to fluctuate and the oil quantity started to deplete rapidly. Mindful that the SR-71 is not renowned for its two-engine out gliding abilities, the pilot attempted a restart on the shutdown right engine. Although successful, the young pilot really had his hands full as the right engine continued to compressor stall and the left engine began to surge.

With the right engine providing hydraulic pressure for the flight controls, but little in the way of additional thrust, heavy vapour was seen coming from the left engine by observers near the runway's end. With zero oil pressure and engine RPM unwinding rapidly towards idle, the left engine was in the final stages of flameout and beginning to seize-up. The pilot chopped the left throttle, held the nose straight with thrust-opposing rudder force, and landed using the right engine. On touchdown he shut down the right engine to prevent damage from over temperature.

On another occasion, the same crew were in the thick of it again. During the acceleration phase to Mach 3 plus, the altitude director light failed, resulting in an air abort. The pilot observed a fuel flow imbalance during the deceleration and levelling off at FL310, both he and his RSO saw a large fire engulf the engine nacelle and spread over the wing and up to the vertical tail section. Immediately after shutting down the engine and pulling the emergency fuel cut off switch, the RPM and EGT decreased— but the fire remained. Increasing airspeed to blow out the fire, the pilot's next priority was to prepare the aircraft for an emergency landing at the nearest suitable airfield. He began emergency fuel dumping and selected afterburner on the remaining engine to descend through some poor weather conditions as quickly as possible. Another successful single-engined landing was made at the chosen alternate!

In addition to their operational duties crews have undertaken other reconnaissance tasks. In 1975 an SR-71 tried to locate the wreckage of a Cessna 310 near Anchorage, Alaska. The twin engined aircraft had disappeared along with its pilot, and passengers Senator Hale Boggs, Republican Nick Begich, and his aide Russell Brown. Unfortunately, no trace was ever found.

During the eruption of Mount St Helens on 18 May 1980 two SR-71s photographed the area to help search and rescue and disaster relief efforts and to record the vast eastward ashfall across Oregon, Washington, Idaho and Montana.

Following the downfall of the dictator Samosa in Nicaragua and the establishment of a Marxist government, Soviet military aid was requested. In the Autumn of 1984, the team of US 'crateologists' were again interested in the cargo on a Soviet freighter that had docked in Nicaragua. The photographs, taken by a US reconnaissance satellite, showed what they believed were MiG-21 interceptors. Nicaragua denied that the crates contained MiGs and maintained that the cargo consisted of Mi-8 helicopters.

After clearance from the White House, four or five SR-71 missions were flown over Nicaragua from Beale. The first sortie was flown on 7 November 1984, and the final one four days later. As a result of reconnaissance and correlative intelligence the MiG-21/helicopter wrangle slowly faded from the head-

lines along with rumours of a possible US invasion of Nicaragua. Some months later, the world's Press confirmed that no MiG-21s had, or were, being supplied to Nicaragua. Reports of crated MiGs issued by the US State Department were pure invention.

This finely-tuned piece of surveillance apparatus would be of little value were it not for the dedication and professionalism of the ground crews who maintain it.

The unique operational, structural, and propulsion aspects of the SR-71 impose maintenance demands unrivalled by any other aircraft. Now 20 years old, a major concern is the availability of spares. Many of the original SR-71 suppliers have either gone out of business or are no longer producing the necessary items. A prime example of this problem can be seen in support of the Pratt & Whitney J58 engine. Ten years ago, engines going into the shop for major inspection were being turned around in about 15 days, despite a more stringent inspection criteria. Today the turnround time ranges from one month to six weeks.

There is at least one case on record of a J58 eventually being re-installed in an aircraft after having spent more than a year in the maintenance shop due to parts shortages. Such problems have caused Det 6 at Norton AFB, to contract out for many of the necessary spares.

The aircraft demands tender loving care from maintenance personnel, involving hundreds of maintenance man-hours per flight—compared with 30–40 for the KC-135 tanker. With experience gained over the years, the list of 875 items to be checked during post flight inspection has been reduced to 650. Even so, it still takes a team of five specialists about six hours to complete the inspection which includes an examination of every titanium and plastic spot weld on the top of the wing!

More extensive inspections and maintenance actions are undertaken after every 25 and 50 hours of flight time, with major inspections and repairs occuring every 100 and 200-hours.

Inlet centrebody spikes are removed during every 50-hour check, allowing close inspection by struc-

The original photograph of SR-71B 64-17956 flying its 1000th sortie. Twin ventral fins are fitted to the two-seat trainer to compensate for the loss of directional stability caused by the raised cockpit (Lockheed-California)

tural specialists. After these spikes are removed, work in the inlet duct often requires the removal of the engine because of very limited work space.

The 100-hour inspection normally takes about 11 working days, each consisting of 16 hours. This inspection often incorporates any field-level modifications. A specialized analysis cart, known as a 'hot gig', is used when trouble-shooting the hydraulic system. By duplicating on the ground the actual hydraulic fluid temperatures reached during high-speed cruise, the 'hot gig' enables the detection of small leaks that would normally go unseen at ambient ground temperatures—hot fluid leaks emit small puffs of vapourized hydraulic fluid.

Two-hundred hour inspections, programmed to take about 15 days, normally take around a month to complete. Every component in the aircraft (including the engines) is stripped down and inspected, many items being replaced. Because of extreme temperature variation the fuel cell seals crack; the sealant is removed and replaced. The J58 engines are removed and returned to Pratt & Whitney for a complete overhaul after 600 hours of operation. Removal from the aircraft involves raising the hinged outer wing nacelle unit. An elaborate hydraulically controlled 'dolly' is used by five technicians to carefully draw the engine from the rear nacelle. It is estimated that between six to nine hours are required to re-install a J58. Every three years SR-71s are rotated through Palmdale for a complete teardown, overhaul, and update known throughout the aircraft world as inspection and repair as necessary (IRAN). The aircraft returns to flying 'almost new'.

A shortage of career 'blue suit' personnel has threatened the continuity of SR-71 maintenance schedules. This problem was caused in the sixties and seventies by the low retention rates of highly qualified men. With four-year enlistees coming to Beale directly from Air Force technical training schools, each trainee had to undergo an additional 18 to 24 months of on the job training before they were qualified to work without constant supervision. This long apprenticeship left only 18 months for these technicians to be fully utilized before leaving the service. The resultant lower experience levels manifested themselves in an overall increase in the maintenance man-hours per SR-71 flight hour. To help redress this growing problem and to provide long-term continuity within the SR-71 maintenance effort, civilian field service workers were employed. According to the Air Force, they provided exceptional value for money.

But in the eighties, the US Air Force no longer had a retention problem and many skilled technicians stayed in, while others who left the ranks joined the contractor-supported operations at improved rates of pay, insuring that high-investment skills were still on hand. Consequently, many of those who now 'keep 'em flying' are 'old heads' who have years of Habu support experience. Born of such long-term dedication, military and civilian esprit de corps is exemplified by the 9th SRW's motto: Semper Paratus—always ready.

Chapter 6
SR-71 Operations 2
The Habu Enigma

In the late sixties the war in Vietnam continued to escalate. Because the U-2 was considered vulnerable in a high threat area it was decided that the SR-71 would also be deployed in support. In mid-1968, four aircraft, among them numbers, '974, '976 and '978 were sent with crews and supporting equipment to Kadena Air Base on the island of Okinawa in Japan.

When the Japanese residents of the islands saw the long sleek aircraft for the first time they named the Blackbird 'Habu'. A Habu is a poisonous pit viper that is found on the Ryuku islands. Though non-aggressive, the small, dark snake can inflict a painful and sometimes deadly bite. 'Habu' has long been the most popular nickname for the SR-71 amongst the crews who fly the aircraft and people closely associated with it over the years since early operations from Okinawa. (Note: most US Air Force aircraft have official nicknames that the world is generally familiar with. In some cases aircraft only have unofficial nicknames. The SR-71 has never been named but it is popularly known as the 'Blackbird', a name ignored by the inner circle. Although resisted by officialdom the name 'Habu' appears to be permanent).

Ferrying the aircraft across the Pacific to Kadena took about five hours. Departing Beale loaded with 65,000 lb (29,545 kg) of fuel, the aircraft would dash to 70,000 ft (21,341 km) to test the inlets before risking 7,000 miles (12,963 km) of ocean with few alternative landing fields. After an initial refuelling 1,000 miles (1852 km) west of San Francisco the aircraft would then be flown on a direct track for Midway beyond the Hawaiian Islands for a second refuelling. After refuelling the SR-71 would then be flown directly to Kadena, where another tanker would be waiting on the ground ready to launch should more fuel be required for emergency or diversionary needs. With four aircraft from Beale at this West Pacific outpost, Detachment (Det) 1 of the 9th SRW was born. Crews used the 'Oxcart flight test' operations building which was most desirable

for away-from-home maintenance of a demanding new aircraft. Built to support the first year A-12 operations, the building was eventually given over to the 'blue suiters', but overseas temporary accomodation for the aeroplanes was initially found in old hangars in the middle of the airfield, known as the 'Little Creek' area. Soon the three primary aircraft were flown regularly with a fourth serving as a 'warm spare'.

During the deployment known as 'Giant Reach' the crews served in Southeast Asia on a temporary duty cycle (TDY) lasting 70 days. On each crew's arrival at Kadena, they would fly a short local orientation flight to familiarize themselves with the airfield and area.

During early operations the aircraft experienced occasional electrical failures. Generator losses resulted in several diversions into US airfields at Utapao and Korat in Thailand and into Danang in South Vietnam and on transpacific ferry flight from Beale to Kadena, an aircrew was forced to land at Midway Island for the same reason. In that case, a new generator was installed and their flight was completed a week later.

The first SR-71 operational mission over Vietnam was flown in April 1968 by crew E-10 Maj Jerome F O'Malley and his RSO Maj Edward Payne. After that initial flight, missions were flown from one to three times a week over Vietnam. Operational flights from Kadena normally departed between 10:00 and 14:00 hr, depending on the angle of the sun over the collection area for shadow length. Twenty minutes after take-off the first AR would take place. A full load of fuel would be taken onboard, and the SR-71 would accelerate to cruise Mach and altitude heading south-westwards. Flying in international airspace between Taiwan to the north and Luzon to the south, the Habu would accelerate to high Mach to round the south coast of the Hainan Islands to enter the Gulf of Tonkin northbound. The penetration point of North

169

SR-71A 64-17974 was loaned to Det 6 at Palmdale by the 9th SRW while '955 was down for extended maintenance and modifications—hence the Lockheed 'Skunk Works' emblem
(via Paul F Crickmore)

Vietnamese airspace would depend upon intelligence requirements, but often this would be in the Haiphong area, and would continue westwards over Hanoi, through Laotian airspace and into Thailand. The nearest, it has been said, the SR-71 has been allowed to fly to China was 12 nautical miles (22 km), which would allow an oblique camera view as it entered a prolonged turn to overfly Laos. Descending into Thailand, a second aerial refuelling would take place, southbound from two tankers orbiting near Korat airbase.

Punching off this tanker, the SR-71 pilot would climb his aircraft back to altitudes above 75,000 ft (22,866 m) accelerating to cruise Mach. Turning east and entering the Gulf of Tonkin once again another reconnaissance run would be flown with the penetration point displaced to the south or north to collect data from a different area. On reaching Thailand, a third AR would take place and a final climb out would be made, on a direct track back towards Kadena. Typically a mission of this type would last about $5\frac{1}{2}$ hours and cover nearly 7,000 miles (12,693 km).

Occasionally, the weather patterns existing in the Southeast Asian region favoured the type of photography carried out by the SR-71s long focal length systems. Large tropical circulation patterns could draw much of the moisture away from land masses and out over the South China Sea, creating clear skies for the cameras to maximize photographic resolution. Over Southeast Asia, clouds could form above 65,000 ft (19,817 m) and despite its ability to fly well above normal build ups, the SR-71 could have its usually rock-solid ride disrupted by the convected instability within tall thunderstorms hidden in high cirrus clouds.

Mission payloads would usually consist of an OBC nose and tech. cameras. Each flight would obtain imagery from literally hundreds of targets which covered everything from supply depots, harbour

installations and industrial complexes to POW camps. SR-71s supplied photographic intelligence for 'Operation Kingpin', the attempted rescue of US POWs from Son Tay prison camp in North Vietnam.

During these routine Southeast Asian sorties, many attempts were made by the North Vietnamese to shoot down a SR-71. All failed. On more than one occasion, a concerted effort was mounted to bag a Habu. Many SA-2s were fired but they all missed! After hundreds of wasted SA-2s, the Vietnamese and their Soviet advisors seemed to lose heart and did not try to strike at one for a long time. With ample warning the RSO was able to bring to bear highly effective electronic defence systems.

With downward visibility from the cockpit position limited by the small windows and wide chines, the RSO has a small viewsight positioned in the underside to keep a visual check of the aircraft's position. This viewsight together with the pilot's small rearward facing periscope (situated on the top of the canopy) gave some crews a most interesting spectacle when fired upon by a missile. As the explosion billowed out behind, the burst would appear to implode or collapse almost instantly

Main wheels chocked, SR-71A 64-17961 performs engine run-up tests on the 'hammerhead' at Kadena, Japan, in January 1974.
(Dick Gerdes via Robert F Dorr)

because of the SR-71's speed away from the explosion.

After recovery at Kadena, data collected during the flight was taken to the mobile processing center. The MPC is an air-deployable complex consisting of ten vans which provide high-speed film and data processing and communications.

Wet interpretation of photographic material is carried out in the MPC by skilled 'Recce-tech' personnel. Much of the data is then communicated to Headquarters Pacific Air Force (PACAF) at Hickam AFB, Hawaii. Deeper analysis is further carried out by civilians at the National Photo Interpretation Center in Washington. The MPC can process film at 160 ft (49 m) per minute, after which four prints or

TOP LEFT
CMSgt Bill Gornick prepares his famous tie-cutting ceremony with a mini-samurai sword for the crew of an SR-71 after an operational mission over North Vietnam

TOP RIGHT
An impressive array of Habu mission marks; each snake represents an operational mission over North Vietnam (Lockheed-California)

Det 1 deployed to Kadena in 1968 and the first operational flight of an SR-71 (or 'Habu') over Southeast Asia took place in April that same year. In pressure suits, Maj Haupt (left) and RSO Maj Boynton appear to be enduring some good natured jibes from their 1st SRS colleagues

more are made from one negative to be dispatched to users.

After operational missions over North Vietnam, white snake symbols in the form of a minature Habu were applied beneath the cockpit like kill symbols. As time passed, SR-71s deployed to that theatre were soon sporting a very respectable number of white Habus; unfortunately they were ordered to be removed because critics felt that the symbols 'told too much'.

On 1 November 1968, the Secretary of the Air Force notified the Strategic Air Command that the 9th SRW was to be awarded the Air Forces' Outstanding Unit Award. The citation to accompany that award reads 'The 9th SRW, Beale AFB, California, distinguished itself by exceptionally meritorious services to the USAF during the period 1 July 1967 to 30 June 1968. By the successful completion of final testing and evaluation of the SR-71 aircraft and execution of Strategic Reconnaissance Operations on a global scale. Essentially pioneering the concept of sustained supersonic flight by a manned weapons system, the officers and airmen of the 9th SRW, by their dedication, initiative and devotion to duty significantly contributed to the growing aerospace age and the cause of peace, thereby reflecting great credit upon themselves, the Strategic Air Command and the United States Air Force.'

Most of the crews that pioneered these early operational missions were awarded the Distinguished Flying Cross (DFC) for important new achievements in flight. As time went by this award was given for especially significant target imagery. A typical citation for such flights is found in Maj John Storrie's award, which reads . . . 'for his extraordinary achievement whilst participating in aerial flight on a highly sensitive, special catagory reconnaissance mission on 22 May 1968'.

Two SR-71s were lost whilst operating from Det 1 at Kadena. The first (17969) occurred in the early seventies during an operational mission against North Vietnam. Shortly after air refuelling, the pilot initiated a normal full power climb. Stretching before him was a solid bank of cloud containing heavy thunderstorm activity which reached above 40–45,000 ft (12,195–13,719 m). Easing the nose into a high angle of attack at between Mach 0.8 and 0.9, the pilot intended to climb over a saddleback of clouds between the build-ups and stay clear of the weather. Heavy with fuel, the aircraft was unable to sustain this higher climb attitude and as the aircraft entered turbulence both engines flamed out. With the pilots attention fully occupied with maintaining control, the engine RPM reduced to the point where restarts were impossible. Both crew members ejected shortly after the aircraft stalled. It hit the ground near Korat in Thailand.

The other loss was the famous 'Rapid Rabbit', a late-production aircraft which accumulated more SEA sorties than any other SR-71. In May 1973, '978

was returning to base after a successful operational mission. Although high winds were blowing over Kadena's east/west runways, it was decided to attempt a maximum crosswind landing.

In marginal landing conditions, a practice had been adopted for safe brake parachute use on the SR-71; the big 'rapid 'chute' was jettisoned as soon as the initial effect had taken a heavy 'bite' of the aircraft's momentum.

'Rapid' deploy-jettison was employed to prevent the large 'chute from sharply weather-cocking the aircraft directly into wind and pulling it off the side of the runway. This procedure was being followed, but the pilot, unhappy with the touchdown, elected to 'go-around' and applied full power for another attempt.

Touching down this time without a brake 'chute and slightly 'hot', 'Rapid Rabbit' lived up to its name. The pilot was unable to keep '978 on the runway. One of the wheel trucks hit the concrete barrier housing, which badly damaged the gear and caused substantial additional damage to the aircraft. Both crew members clambered out unscathed, but after an extensive evaluation technicians and commanders decided to write-off the fastest Rabbit in the world. The famous playboy logo never appeared again on a Habu. Number '978 was subsequently broken up for spares.

On 24 September 1974, a newly qualified combat-ready crew got airborne from Kadena for a Functional Check Flight (FCF). Descending through 77,000 ft (23,476 m) and in excess of Mach 3, a fourth stage compressor blade disintegrated causing shrapnel damage to the engine casing and nacelle. The thrown blade severed both oil and hydraulic lines causing an intense fire in the right engine nacelle. The loss of thrust and immediate high drag condition which accompanied the engine failure created sudden pitch, roll, and yaw oscillations which took the aircraft to the brink of its stability limits. During the emergency descent, the left engine also flamed out leaving the aircraft with only battery power for its systems. Engine and airframe vibrations temporarily became so severe that the crew members were buffeted about the cockpit to the degree that made it impossible to read either the instruments or check lists. Loss of cabin pressurization caused the crews' pressure suits to inflate, further hampering their freedom of movement. Despite these difficulties the pilot was able to shutdown the right engine, extinguish the fire, and airstart the left engine. The aircraft was recovered on the single engine without further incident.

On 25 April 1975 an experienced crew, (Capt Robert C Helt and his RSO Maj Larry Elliott) came close to losing an aircraft from Kadena. Flying on an operational sortie they suffered a series of multiple emergencies. First they lost an engine. With it went both hydraulic systems, half the electrical system, and the primary navigation system. Flying several

Identified by the Playboy bunny motif on the fin, 'Rapid Rabbit', SR-71A 64-17978, was written off after a spectacular landing accident at Kadena in May 1973. The crew were unharmed
(US Air Force via Gary Baker)

hundred miles from land and unable to get the engine restarted the crew members had their hands full. At the same time, the aircraft developed a severe fuel leak. Despite all of these problems the crew worked smoothly to bring the aircraft safely back to Kadena. For his actions Capt Helt was presented with the Karen Kolligan Trophy, a highly respected award. Established in 1958 to recognise annually the most outstanding feat of airmanship in the US Air Force for that year, by an individual crew member who averted an aircraft accident.

With Richard Nixon elected to the Presidency on 20 January 1969 he brought with him a promise of 'Peace with Honour', in Vietnam. Soon a slow withdrawal of US forces from the war zone began. To ensure against 'Protective Reaction Strikes', during the 1972 and 73 bombing halts (North Vietnam fired upon reconnaissance aircraft). Nixon ordered a temporary ban on all flights over North Vietnam including manned reconnaissance to preserve the fragile Paris peace negotiations. The flight profile of the SR-71 was altered dramatically. Instead of simple northbound overflights, a tight-turn sortie was repeatedly flown within the Gulf of Tonkin and the SR-71 had to remain off the coast of North Vietnam to gather all reconnaissance data from a stand-off vantage point. To stay within the restrictive confines of the Gulf, it was necessary to fly at a reduced altitude and Mach. At FL 750 and below it was possible to sustain a steep turn without reducing speed below Mach 3.

The in-country war in Vietnam ended for the United States when the Paris agreement was signed on 27 January 1973, commiting withdrawal of US forces from South Vietnam. In addition, the agreement included the release of US prisoners within 60 days, the formation of a Four Party Joint Military Mission, the establishment of an International Commission of Control and Supervision, the clearance of mines from NVN waters, and for free elections by all Vietnamese. For the SR-71, it meant a return to routine stand-off reconnaissance flights, respecting the newly 'united' north-dominated Vietnam.

Within the operational sphere of Det 1s interest is North Korea. With regular border incursions by North Korean intruders and with a sensitive 'balance' along the 38th parallel, the United States is eager to avoid another bloody confrontation. The SR-71, using stand-off techniques employing long-

'Rapid Rabbit' in happier days refuelling from a KC-135Q

range oblique cameras, can gather high quality photo reconnaissance for regular analysis. Certain important categories of intelligence are made available to the Commander-in-Chief, United Nations Command, Korea (CINCUNC). North Korean representatives at the UN claim these flights violate their airspace.

On 1 November 1977, an experienced crew were scheduled to fly a routine Korean monitoring sortie. Airborne from Kadena in '961, about 1 hr 20 min into the flight and entering a sensitive area, the right inlet control system suffered a catastrophic hydraulic failure. In a programmed 30° left banked turn the right engine inlet controls 'unstarted', forcing the aircraft into a hard right-bank which threatened to take them into North Korean airspace. Immediately, the pilot applied hard left stick to regain the left bank and track control. At the same time, it was necessary to initiate emergency descent procedures. Subsequently, the disrupted airflow caused the right engine to flame out. As the airplane continued its yawing and vibrating descent, further inlet disturbances caused the left engine to also flame out. From the moment of the initial hydraulic failure to double-engine flame out, a period of less than ten seconds had elapsed. Descending rapidly without power towards the emergency recovery airfield, the pilot was able to restart the left engine again as he descended through 63,000 ft (19,207 m). Despite continued efforts the right engine was not restarted until the aircraft had reached subsonic flight at FL290. With power now restored to both engines, the crew successfully recovered the aircraft to Osan in South Korea. The exceptional flying skill of an experienced pilot avoided an international incident and saved a valuable aircraft.

In a broadcast from radio Pyongyang on Friday 12 December 1980, North Korea claimed that an SR-71 had crossed the Demilitarized Zone (DMZ) near Kosong, just north of the 38th parallel. These allegations were strenuously denied by the United States.

On Saturday, 20 June 1981, another Pyongyang broadcast alleged that an SR-71 violated their airspace the previous day in the same area. The broadcast went on to claim more than 70 violations of North Korean airspace by SR-71s in the first six months of that year; this would put the number of incursions at three a week.

A fine study of SR-71A 64-17980 taken by the camera of a Jaguar strike aircraft from No 41 Sqn, RAF, based at Coltishall in Norfolk, England (Crown copyright)

But the matter of incursions escalated on Wednesday, 26 August, when an SR-71 reported to be in South Korean airspace was fired at by a North Korean SAM site. The crew of the SR-71 reported sighting a rocket contrail and a subsequent air burst several miles distant.

Secretary of Defense Caspar Weinberger informed the President of the incident. State Department spokesman, Dean Fischer, said 'The Reagan Administration roundly denounces this act of lawlessness' and that the attack violated 'accepted norms of international behavior.' The North Koreans later denied the missile charge. As the year wore on, North Korea continued to claim that SR-71s were violating their airspace. These accusations led Lt Cdr Mark Brender of the Defense Department to state 'We have continued to fly our (reconnaissance) missions since the 26 August shooting incident. They take place over South Korea and in international airspace. They do not fly over the North.' The latest alleged SR-71 incursion resulted in the North calling the 408th

TOP RIGHT
*SR-71A 64-17974 turns for the barn at the end of a
mission
(Kevin Gothard)*

Brake 'chute discarded, SR-71A 64-17974 continues its
roll out down runway 29 at Mildenhall
(Kevin Gothard)

TOP LEFT
*The inlet spikes point down slightly by $5\frac{1}{2}°$ and toe in $3°$ to
achieve the optimum level of airflow alignment into the
engines
(Kevin Gothard)*

meeting of the North Korean Military Armistice
Commission, in the truce village of Panmunjom. At
the meeting, the senior North Korean delegate, Maj
General Han Ju-Kyong, said this of the SR-71
flights: 'These premeditated, provocative acts ag-
gravate the situation on the Korean peninsula to a
high pitch of strain. You should know there is a limit
to our patience'. Representing the United Nations
Command. US Rear Admiral James G Stroms III,
retorted, 'I remind your side not to underestimate
our resolve on this matter. These routine flights are so
carefully controlled, that there is no chance they will
violate your legal airspace'. The flights continue from
Kadena despite the protestations of North Korea.

Activated in March 1979 at RAF Mildenhall,
Suffolk, Det 4 was a U-2R detachment from the
reactivated 99th SRS Beale AFB. Under the mission
title 'Senior Ruby', their task was to obtain Elint and
Comint.

Using the callsign 'BURNS 31', 17972 arrived at
Mildenhall on 20 April 1976. Its ten day TDY stint
marked the beginning of a steady build up of SR-71
operations from this East Anglian base, which by
early 1980 had expanded to boast a purpose-built
hangar. U-2 operations from Mildenhall declined
and were eventually moved to RAF Alconbury,
where an expanded TR-1 unit was formed to
continue these vital tasks.

On 5 April 1984 Prime Minister Margaret
Thatcher announced that a detachment of SR-71s

Taken over East Anglia, England, in the spring of 1982 by Sqn Ldr Allan Mathie using the F.95 Mk 10 camera of his Jaguar, Flt Lt Derek Bridge (also Jaguar mounted) formates with SR-71A '980 crewed by Maj Nevin Cunningham and RSO Maj Gene Quist (Crown copyright)

had been formed at RAF Mildenhall. A blanket clearance to operate two SR-71s in the United Kingdom was granted by the government. That clearance replaced the earlier limited duration one clearance, one aircraft agreement.

Expansion followed smoothly as new facilities and longer serving personnel were added. Today the detachment consists of about ten officers, 80 enlisted personnel and 50 technical support civilians (employed primarily by Lockheed and Pratt & Whitney). Aircrew members, however, continue to man the Det, on a 45-day temporary duty basis.

Following a much needed cash injection for new central facilities, the formerly dispersed operation came together into a single, large, new facility. Two new hangar barns (first used on 8 August 1985 by '962) feature roll-in roll-out access and a plumbed-in air system for engine startup.

Missions flown from Mildenhall can be broken down into two main operational areas: one 'north' and the other 'south'. The vast majority of these operations are flown to the north. Under such mission titles as 'Viking North' etc, these stand-off flights constitute an important part of the peacetime aerial reconnaissance programme (Parpro). The term 'Sierra' flight is used in RAF circles when refering to SR-71 operations, which are conducted, of necessity, under conditions of pre-mission secrecy. Specific tracks relating to the aircraft's movements within Europe are classified as NATO Secret.

A typical SR-71 sortie to the north might unfold as follows: a few hours before the flight a coded message would go out to all of the Air Traffic Service Units (ATSUs) affected by the flight which need to know of its existence. About one hour before the SR-71 departs, two or three KC-135Q tankers launch to make their way to refuelling tracks near Norway. Initially controlled by Eastern radar, the tankers are then handed over to Border radar. On reaching a point 60° north, the tankers then proceed using 'Visual Flight Rules'. This 'VFR' movement ensures that the element of surprise is maintained, as the aircraft's position is not reported and aircrews no longer have to make or answer radio calls.

Before the SR-71s departure, another KC-135 leaves. WOrking with Eastern radar, this tanker proceeds to a holding pattern off the north Norfolk coast, and 'holds' at FL 260. Operating in radio

*Oozing JP-7 from its full tanks, SR-71A, callsign 'MINTY 23', disengages from the flying boom before it slips gently away to the right (above) to clear KC-135Q 'EQUAL 61' on 6 October 1981
(Paul F Crickmore)*

silence, the SR-71 has absolute priority. With all other air traffic delayed, the SR-71 is cleared to take off when ready. Takeoff is executed exactly on the scheduled departure time. Using a radio callsign known to the air traffic control agencies which 'work' the mission, the Blackbird goes to work. Callsigns change often for security reasons.

In order to establish that the aircraft has two-way communication with the ground, it uses its IFF (identification friend or foe) transponder when directed by air traffic control (ATC) to 'squawk ident'. ATC can then verify that all is well by a discrete secondary surveillance radar (SSR) code which pulses the radar return on the controller's radar display. Should it be necessary to 'control' the SR-71 to avoid other aircraft, the controller will direct the aircraft as necessary but will not receive the read back of instructions demanded from other flights. Climbing like the proverbial 'bat out of hell', the SR-71 reaches FL260 in about four minutes, levels off and makes for the tanker holding northeast of The Wash. Once linked to the tanker, the two aircraft proceed in a NNE direction. With the first AR completed off Flamborough Head, the tanker recovers back to Mildenhall as the SR-71 lights its afterburners and blasts off to the northeast.

Rounding northern Norway, stand-off reconnaissance tracks are flown to monitor strategic targets

SR-71A in the roll-out phase being decelerated by the 49 ft (15 m) diameter braking parachute. The control tower at RAF Mildenhall is in the background (Paul F Crickmore)

LEFT
The SR-71 uses a three-stage brake parachute system: after the doors are open a small 'chute removes an outer cover, followed by a large drogue 'chute (pictured) which deploys the main canopy (Paul F Crickmore)

along the northern coast of the Soviet Union. Flying 17 miles (30 km) high and remaining outside the internationally recognized 12 mile (22 km) limit, the optical systems onboard can reveal deeper targets some 75–80 miles (138–148 km) inland. Turning back to the west, the SR-71 swings once more over the Norwegian Sea and flies down the coast to rendezvous with other KC-135s. Tanking to the brim until fuel vents from every tiny leak, the aircraft then accelerates away from the tanker, which returns to Mildenhall.

Back at Mach 3.0 and 80,000 ft (24,390 m) the SR-71 (having acquired NATO overflight clearance of Denmark before the flight) enters the Baltic Sea area. Remaining clear of Polish and Soviet airspace, the aircraft runs up the coast of both countries to a point to the east of the northern tip of Gotland. It then swings in a 120 mile (222 km) diameter circle, through 180°, before flying down the narrow corridor of international airspace that exists between Gotland and Oland. Swedish Air Force Saab JA-37 Viggen interceptors sometimes seize upon the opportunity for a chance to practice high-speed, high-altitude interception. Airborne from their base at Norkoping, the 13th Wing have realized that the only way of attacking such a high-speed target is a collision course 'snap-up' attack. Swedish pilots have unofficially claimed radar lock-ons and visual sightings of the Blackbird during Mach 5 closure between the two aircraft. Such claims (if true) demonstrate not only the exceptional skill of the Swedish pilots, and their GCI controllers, but also speaks highly of the JA-37s pulse-Doppler radar.

After clearing the Baltic area via the same route 30 minutes after entering it, the SR-71 heads for home. The RSO ensures that the aircraft returns to UK airspace at the correct re-entry point, at the appointed time, and squawking the proper ident code to ensure positive identification by the UK air defence staff at Nettishead. While descending through 60,000 ft (18,300 m), the RSO switches the Mode 'Charlie' altitude readout back on for the benefit of air traffic controllers. With the mission all but over restrictions are relaxed and the SR-71 approaches Mildenhall just like any fighter-type aircraft to make a 'run and break' or 'pitch out' before landing. A typical northern mission lasts four hours.

Missions flown to the south are longer, usually five hours. Before departure a NATO-like diplomatic clearance is obtained from France. Two tankers from Mildenhall fly on civil airways through France to the Mediterranean area. On rare occasions the tankers land at Sigonella, to ground refuel before returning to Mildenhall. Forty minutes after the first KC-135 departs, another tanker gets airborne at Mildenhall and makes for The Wash area holding pattern. About 30 min after that, the SR-71 launches and climbs to refuel at FL260 from a tanker over the North Sea. Climbing to a high cruising level, the SR-71 keeps to international waters over the Atlantic, entering the Mediterranean Sea from the west. Descent is made to RV with the two tankers for a second AR. This track runs easterly and is located to the south of Sicily. Back at Mildenhall, a fourth tanker leaves about one hour after the SR-71, flying General Air Traffic (GAT) routes southeast to take up a holding station along an AR route in the western Mediterranean.

The AR task completed, and having reached cruise altitude and speed it is thought likely that the SR-71 takes a stand-off look at Libya before turning north. Cleared to overfly Turkey, it is highly probable that

TOP LEFT/RIGHT
The brake 'chute doors remain open as the Habu taxies
back to its lair
(Paul F Crickmore)

the airplane enters the Black Sea area to soak up the wide range of data accessible from this important operating area. Stocks of JP-7 are held in storage at an undisclosed location if it becomes necessary to divert for any reason. Egressing from a collection area, the Habu heads for its third aerial refuelling. After top-off, it heads north easterly to land back at Mildenhall. About thirty minutes before scheduled landing time, a fifth tanker is crewed-up as ground spare to launch if the SR-71 needs more fuel for emergency or precautionary reasons.

On Saturday, 19 January 1985, an SR-71 took part in Exercise Cold Fire, a NATO exercise then in full swing in Germany. At 07:30 local, the crew left Mildenhall's runway 11 in OVIS 20 and headed for The Wash and fuel. After routine aerial refuelling the SR-71 accelerated to Mach 2.8 and climbed to maintain 75,000 ft (22,866 m). Flying at this reduced speed reduces the radius of turn monoeuvring within the limited confines of friendly airspace in southern Germany. The reduced flight level significantly increases fuel consumption. Levelling off over the North Sea, OVIS 20 coasted in over northern Germany. Flying in steeper turns at this constant but reduced speed and altitude is very demanding for the pilot. With an outside air temperature of about −65°C, the CIT is at a lower temperature than usual, and the aircraft wants to fly faster. Retarding the throttles causes the airplane to ease into a slight descent. Skill and experience is therefore demanded of the pilot to maintain the tight profile. Having flown over the 'waring' forces and reached a point just south of Munchen, the pilot eased OVIS 20 through 180° to fly back up through Germany, across the North Sea and down again onto the boom of the waiting second tanker. Tanking completed, the whole flight profile

SECOND FROM TOP
Parked on the ramp at Mildenhall, an SR-71 is checked
for any obvious problems by the ground crew. The twin fins
are canted 15° inboard at the tip to reduce the rolling
moment due to sideslip and vertical deflection
(Paul F Crickmore)

ABOVE
A mission that did not go according to plan: 64-17974
returned to Mildenhall 30 minutes after takeoff with a
technical problem
(Kevin Gothard)

Combustion chambers aglow, SR-71 64-17979 taxies out for an early morning departure in damp weather conditions (Paul F Crickmore)

SR-71 64-17974 swings on to runway 11 at Mildenhall to lineup and hold prior to takeoff (Kevin Gothard)

RIGHT
An SR-71A refuelling from a McDonnell Douglas KC-10A Extender: this versatile tanker/cargo aircraft made its operational debut during Operation Eldorado Canyon, the American bombing raid against Libya on 15 April 1986

was repeated a second time. Landing back at 'The Hall' at 11:30, this four-hour mission was flown with a radar nose. The bad weather conditions prevailing over Europe ensured that photography was of little use.

One week later 17979, callsign 'OIL 54', was flown on an identical sortie. The pilot for this trip was formally a member of the Thunderbirds display team. This second flight allowed a comparative analysis to be made with the data acquired from the previous mission. Highly qualified interpreters form a picture of significant military and industrial capability in order to predict how, and in what areas, such power might be used.

In any theatre of operations, intelligence planners at Mildenhall, Kadena, or Beale, are given a list of priority targets. This list would have been compiled as a result of intelligence requirements generated by the Defense Intelligence Agency (DIA), Central Intelligence Agency (CIA), and the US State Department. A rough route to cover as many of these targets as possible is then drawn up and handed to the route planners. These highly skilled planners (usually very experienced navigators) work out precise route details while taking into account the targets to be covered, the aircraft's operating weight, speed, altitude and bank angles. Additionally, the aerial refuelling requirements are calculated to

include such factors as tanker range, the SR-71s single-engine fuel range, missed refuelling alternate bases, etc. A certain amount of horse trading goes on between the national intelligence planners and experienced route-planners—the former would like to have 'the aircraft hover at 80,000 ft with an indefinite supply of fuel'. When preliminary planning is completed the entire route is fed into a computer which helps ensure that the designed route has been optimized to take into account all factors and mission requirements.

Dispatched next to SAC HQ, Offutt AFB, the route is replotted and discussed before diplomatic clearances are obtained to enable the aircraft to fly through another friendly nations' airspace. The route is then presented at the Pentagon where representatives from the DIA, CIA, and State Department finally agree on the route structure and target coverage. If the flight violates any airspace, clearance from the highest levels must be obtained first. Depending upon the importance of the mission such permission might come from either the Secretary of Defense, Secretary of State or the President. Every aspect of the programme is extremely tightly controlled, being handled throughout by top specialists in their particular field. A Blackbird operation is something special.

Libya

Following concentrated tanker activity at RAF Mildenhall during the late afternoon, the base became relatively quiet, almost merging into the night. A light south easterly wind and low cloud laden with moderate rain made working conditions unpleasant for ground crews as they laboured to ready the large dark shapes that would provide a spring board for yet another classified Det 4 operation.

At approximately 02:00 hr local, the first of seven tankers cranked up its engines. Shortly afterwards, aided by blue taxiway lights, they picked their way through the night. Stopping short of the active runway, a 'green' from the tower signalled all was clear to lineup and hold on runway 11. With nothing but a wind check from ATC, the tanker's disappeared noisily into the void. The time was 02:40 hr. The date, Tuesday 15 April 1986. World headlines were about to be made.

In all 18 F-111F strike aircraft of the 48th Tactical Fighter Wing (TFW) based at RAF Lakenheath, Suffolk, struck at significant military targets in Libya. The strike force was supported by three EF-111 electronic warfare aircraft of the 42nd Electronic Counter Measures Squadron, 20th TFW, based at RAF Upper Heyford, Oxfordshire, together with 18 KC-10 Extenders and a number of KC-135s.

At approximately 05:00 local, SR-71A 17980 was swallowed up by low clouds as it got airborne from Mildenhall and made for its post-takeoff top up. Once this was completed the aircraft accelerated and climbed away heading due south.

At 06:15, SR-71A 17960 left Mildenhall and duplicated the procedures carried out earlier by its stablemate. Before flying over the collection area it is highly probable that the aircraft refuelled again from the tanker force before accelerating and climbing back up to their operational altitude. With both aircraft configured with panoramic nose sections carrying the Optical Barrel Camera for horizon to horizon coverage, and high-powered frame cameras, their mission was to penetrate Libyan air space and obtain post-strike pictures of the targets hit by the 48th TFW. Post-reconnaissance refuelling was carried out—maybe more than once—during the flight back to Mildenhall.

This particular operation was significant in several respects. Firstly, it was the first occasion that KC-10 aircraft were used to supply tanker support for an operation SR-71 mission from the UK. Secondly, it was the first time that both SR-71s operated by Det 4 have been used together. A carbon copy of this operation—incorporating minor changes for security reasons—was flown on 16/17 April.

The rapid turnround was an outstanding achievement by all concerned.

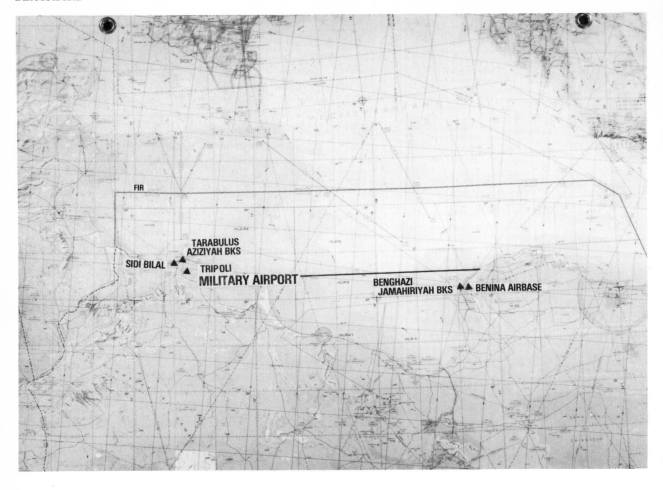

The map used by US Secretary of Defense Caspar
Weinberger at a White House briefing on the bombing
mission against Libya
(Department of Defense)

TOP LEFT
Damage assessment photograph of the havoc inflicted by
US Navy aircraft on Benina Airfield, taken by an SR-71
from Det 4 at Mildenhall on 15 April 1986. A forward
motion compensation unit (FMC) is used to obtain sharp
ground images from the cameras at Mach-3 plus
(Department of Defense)

RIGHT
Libyan Airlines Boeing 727-2L5 (5ADID) was damaged
in the nose section by shrapnel
(Department of Defense)

BENINA AIRFIELD
15 APR 86

DESTROYED MIG-23/FLOGGER

MIG-23/FLOGGER PIECES

BENINA AIRFIELD
15 APR 86

DESTROYED F-27

DAMAGED MI-8/HIP

DESTROYED MI-8/HIP

SR-71A 64-17980, landing light on, gear down, during the 1983 International Air Tattoo at RAF Greenham Common. Before it flew back to Mildenhall, this aircraft was daubed with slogans in protest at the decision to base cruise missiles in the UK
(Paul F Crickmore)

One question certainly begs an answer. Why was it necessary for two SR-71s to be tasked with this mission? The most likely explanation is assured target coverage in the event of an abort or systems malfunction, with perhaps the additional benefit of surprise. As described earlier in this chapter, the SR-71 operates occasionally in this vicinity on an individual basis. To have a second aircraft come storming over the horizon shortly after an earlier aircraft had just left might catch the defences off guard, enabling intelligence to be gathered from an area or system that otherwise might have escaped detection.

But one thing is apparent. Only an aircraft possessing the capabilities of the SR-71 could have possibly carried out such a mission with any chance of success. The operation took place in broad daylight and sophisticated Libyan defence systems were on full alert. These missions proved—if proof were needed—that there's life in the old girl yet.

The close-knit Pilot and RSO team that fly the SR-71 are arguably the most dedicated, professionally competent aircrew in the world. Their aircraft has advanced our understanding of sustained, high-speed, high-altitude flight more than any other. Without peer for over 20 years the SR-71 is a remarkable and unique achievement. If the system is not over-developed and remains cost effective, the airplane will fulfil its role into the 21st century. With military capability and political considerations restricting peacetime SR-71 collection areas, the system continues to provide unique mission flexibility by making a vital contribution to the balanced reconnaissance force of which it is a part. Over the past 20 years, space has become the arena in which overflight activity is politically acceptable—the implementation of President Eisenhower's 'Open Skies' proposal has in effect been accomplished via the back door.

During an American TV interview on *Sixty Minutes*, Kelly Johnson, as sharp and far sighted as ever, had no hesitation in outlining what he sees to be the airplane of the future when he said, '*The best airplane to be designed is going to be the crop duster: it can feed us, it can keep us healthy and help save a country, and a lot of other countries, from starvation*'.

Acknowledgements

One particular individual at Burbank was responsible more than any other for getting this book off the ground; Jeff Fellows. During my week-long stay at the California plant, he co-ordinated interviews with several key individuals intimately connected with the programme and continued to support my research efforts back in the UK. It was therefore with shock and deep regret that I learned of his tragic and untimely death in June 1985.

My editor, Dennis Baldry, also deserves a special word of thanks. It was he, undaunted by the fact that this is my first book and that nobody had ever written an indepth study of the SR-71 before, did not hesitate.

Bob Ferguson and Elsie Martin at Lockheed tirelessly rifled their photographic library on my behalf and pulled out some absolute gems; while Stan Elmer, Norm Crumb and all the staff at Lockheed's Technical Library were of enormous help.

I would also like to thank Dr David Baker, William H Brown, James Eastham, Fitzhugh L Fulton Jr, Robert J Gilliland, Kevin Gothard, Richard P Hallion, Dr Richard Harding, Mike Hirst, Keith Leonard, Graham Luxton, Richmond Miller, Robert F Murphy, William C Park, Benjamin R Rich, Louis W Schalk, William Skliar, William A Weaver, Frederick White and Mike Wilson.

My thanks also go to John Andrews, Kate Armitage, Gary S Baker, Steve and Glynis Barber, R Brian Bell, Robert F Dorr, Rosemary Duval, John Evans, V Mike Farmer, Alan Fletcher, Ray Funk, William Goodliffe, Bill Gunston, Jim and Sue Haight, Mike Hockley, Cheryl Hortel, Don and Anita Jensen, John Jowett, Ed Junkes, Sandra Layton, Clive Leyman, Tony Moore, Dr Nash, Lindsay Peacock, Chris Pocock, Jennifer Reigate, Doug Rough, Joe Rogers, John Simpson, Trevor Stone, Dave Wilton and all the staff at the Royal Aircraft Establishment Farnborough.

For my wife Stephanie,
daughter Nicola and in
memory of
General Jerome F O'Malley

Glossary

AFB   Air Force Base
CIA   Central Intelligence Agency
DIA   Defence Intelligence Agency
ECM   electronic counter measures
ECCM   electronic counter-counter measures
IFF   identification friend or foe

NASA   National Aeronautics and Space Administration
NAS   Naval Air Station
PSD   Physiological Support Division
SAM   surface-to-air missile
Tacan   Tactical air navigation system

Specifications

SR-71A
Type: two-seat strategic reconnaissance aircraft

Powerplant: two Pratt & Whitney J58-1 (JT11D-20) continuous-bleed afterburning turbojets each rated at 32,500 lb (14,742 kg) static thrust at sea level

Performance: maximum speed (also max cruising speed) Mach 3.2 or 2,112 mph (3911 km/h) at 85,000 ft (25,915 m)

Weights: empty 67,500 lb (30,618 kg); gross takeoff 172,000 lb (78,019 kg); maximum fuel capacity 84,180 lb (38,184 kg)

Dimensions: wing span 55.58 ft (16.94 m); wing area 1,795 sq ft (166.82 m²); aspect ratio 1.92; thickness/chord ratio 2.5 per cent; incidence 1.20 degrees; length 103.83 ft (31.65 m); height 18.50 ft (5.64 m)

Armament: none

Appendices

Appendix 1, The Aircraft

A-12/YF-12

60-6924, article number 121. Prototype. Maiden flight 26 April 1962, piloted by Lockheed test pilot Louis W Schalk. In storage at Palmdale.

60-6925, article number 122. Used for ground tests, prior to its first flight. In storage at Palmdale.

60-6926, article number 123. Second A-12 to fly. Lost on 24 May 1963 during routine training flight from Groom Lake. CIA pilot Ken Collins survived.

60-6927, article number 124. Modified to include a raised second cockpit in Q bay. Nicknamed 'Titanium Goose', only pilot trainer version of A-12 built. In storage at Palmdale.

60-6928, article number 125. Lost on 5 January 1967, during a training sortie from Groom Lake. CIA pilot Walt Ray did not survive.

60-6929, article number 126. Lost on 28 December 1967 shortly after takeoff from Groom Lake. CIA pilot Mel Vojvodich ejected safely.

60-6930, article number 127. In storage at Palmdale.

60-6931, article number 128. In storage at Palmdale.

60-6932, article number 129. Lost on 5 June 1968 after inflight emergency during operational mission from Kadena. CIA pilot Jack Weeks killed.

60-6933, article number 130. In storage at Palmdale.

60-6934, article number 1001. Prototype YF-12. First flew 7 August 1963 with test pilot James D Eastham at the controls. Used by Col Robert L Stephens and his FCO Lt Col Daniel Andre in an attempt to establish a new speed and altitude record on 1 May 1965. During the initial run an engine malfunction caused the flight to be aborted. The crew transfered into '936 and obtained both records in this aircraft. Having been placed in storage after the cancellation of the F-12; 1001 transformed into two-seat pilot trainer, redesignated SR-71C and serialled 64-17981. Still operational with the 9th SRW.

60-6935 article number 1002. On completion of the YF-12 test programme, the aircraft placed in storage at Edwards. Taken from retirement, the aircraft flew again on 11 December 1969 and was later made available to NASA and used to investigate the many problems encountered during sustained high-speed, high-altitude flight. After completion of this programme delivered to Wright Patterson AFB, where it is now on permanent display.

60-6936, article number 1003. Following an engine malfunction in '934, '936 was used to obtain all the world speed and altitude records of 1 May 1965. Speed over a straight course of 2070.101 mph and an absolute sustained altitude record of 80,257.86 ft by Col Robert L Stephens and his FCO Lt Col Daniel Andre. Speed record over a closed course of 1,688.889 mph by Lt Col Walter F Daniel and his FCO Maj James P Cooney. Speed record over a 500 km course of 1643.041 mph by Lt Col Walter F Daniel and FCO Maj Noel T Warner. After a brief period of retirement the aircraft was used as part of a joint Air Force and NASA test programme but lost on 24 June 1971.

60-6937, article number 131. In storage at Palmdale.

60-6938, article number 132. In storage at Palmdale.

60-6939, article number 133. Lost on approach to Groom Lake on 9 July 1964. Lockheed test pilot Bill Park ejected safely.

60-6940, article number 134. One of two A-12s converted to carry a launch control officer behind the pilot for D-21 drone operations. This sole surviving example is in storage at Palmdale.

60-6941, article number 135. Second A-12 modified for D-21 operations and lost on 30 July 1966 during a test launch of drone. Its pilot, Bill Park, survived. The Lockheed engineer responsible for launching the drone, Ray Torick, was killed. Serial numbers 60-6942 to 60-6948 were assigned, but not used.

SR-71

64-17950, article number 2001. The prototype. First flew on 22 December 1964. First three aircraft to roll off the line were used by Lockheed as test vehicles. Lost on 10 January 1967 at Edwards AFB, evaluating anti-skid brake system. Lockheed test pilot Art Peterson survived.

64-17951, article number 2002. First flew 3 March 1965. Lockheed gave it to the Air Force in 1969, who made it available to NASA at the Flight Research Center, Edwards AFB on 16 July 1971. Now YF-12C and serialled 60-6937, completed final flight with NASA on 28 September 1978. Lt Col C Jewett and his RSO Maj W Frazier flew the aircraft on 22 December 1978, before it was placed in storage at Palmdale.

64-17952, article number 2003. Used by Lockheed to conduct phase I experimental test flying. Disintegrated during a high-speed, high-altitude test flight on 25 January 1966. Lockheed test pilot Bill Weaver survived but his RSO, Jim Zwayer, killed.

64-17953, article number 2004. Used with '954 and '955 by test pilots from Air Force Systems Command for test and evaluation. Lost on 18 December 1969 after inflight explosion and subsequent high-speed stall. Lt Col Joe Rogers and RSO Lt Col Garry Heidlebaugh ejected safely.

64-17954, article number 2005. Written off on 11 April 1969 at Edwards AFB, after aborted takeoff and fire. Lt Col Bill Skliar and his RSO Maj Noel Warner managed to escape uninjured.

64-17955, article number 2006. Only SR-71A from initial production batch of six still flying. Often pictured with the Lockheed skunk emblazoned upon its tail, it is operated by AFLC at Plant 42, Palmdale.

64-17956, article number 2007. Prototype of two SR-71B two-seat pilot trainers, first flown on 2 November 1965, and delivered to the Air Force on 6 January 1966. Only surviving example of B model and still active.

64-17957, article 2008. Second SR-71B built and delivered to Air Force. Crashed on approch to Beale AFB on 11 January 1968. The instructor pilot Lt Col Robert G Sowers and his 'student' Capt David E Fruehauf survived.

64-17958, article number 2009. First A model delivered to the Air Force, on 10 May 1966. Used on 27/28 July 1976 by Capt Eldon W Joersz and his RSO, Maj George T Morgan Jr to establish the current speed record over a 15/25 kilometre course of 2,193.167 mph. Operational with the 9th SRW.

64-17959, article number 2010. Operational with the 9th SRW.
64-17960, article number 2011. Operational with the 9th SRW.
64-17961, article number 2012. Operational with the 9th SRW.
64-17962, article number 2013.

64-17963, article number 2014. Operational with the 9th SRW.
64-17964, article number 2015.

64-17965, article number 2016. Lost on evening of 25 October 1967 after INS platform failed, leading to erroneous attitude information being displayed in the cockpit. Pilot and RSO ejected safely.
64-17966, article number 2017. Lost on the evening of 13 April 1967 after the aircraft entered a subsonic, high-speed stall. Both crew members ejected safely.
64-17967, article number 2018. Still operational with the 9th SRW.
64-17968, article number 2019. Still operational with the 9th SRW.
64-17969, article number 2020. Lost between 1970 and early 1971 during an operational mission from Kadena. Stalled during post-tanking climb to altitude avoiding bad weather and crashed near Korat RTAFB, Thailand. Pilot and RSO ejected safely.
64-17870, article number 2021. Lost on 17 June 1970 following a post-tanking collision with the KC-135 tanker. Lt Col 'Buddy' Brown and his RSO Maj Mortimer Javis ejected safely. The SR-71 crashed near El Paso, Texas; the KC-135 limped back to Beale with a damaged fin.
64-17971, article number 2022. Operational with the 9th SRW.
64-17972, article number 2023. Used by Maj James Sullivan and his RSO Maj Noel Widdifield to establish a new trans-Atlantic speed record from New York to London in just 1 hour 54 min. 56.4 sec, on 1 September 1974. The same aircraft established yet another world speed record 13 days later, when Capt Harold B Adam and his RSO Maj William C Machorek flew from London to Los Angeles in just 3 hours 47 min 35.8 sec.

64-17973, article number 2024. Operational with the 9th SRW.
64-17974, article number 2025. This aircraft was one of four to undertake first SR-71 operational deployment to Kadena early in 1968. Operational with the 9th SRW.
64-17975, article number 2026. Operational with the 9th SRW.
64-17976, article number 2027. One of four to undertake first SR-71 operational deployment to Kadena early in 1968. Operational with the 9th SRW.
64-17977, article number 2028. Lost on 10 October 1968 following a takeoff abort at Beale on runway 14. Maj James A Kogler was ordered to eject while pilot Maj Gabriel A Kardong elected to stay with the aircraft. Both officers survived.
64-17978, article 2029. This aircraft one of four to undertake first SR-71 operational deployment to Kadena early in 1968. Named the 'Rapid Rabbit', this aircraft was written off sometime in May 1973 at Kadena AB during the roll out phase of its landing. The crew escaped without injury. To-date, this is the last SR-71 to have been written off.
64-17979, article number 2030. Operational with the 9th SRW.
64-17980, article number 2031. Operational with the 9th SRW.
64-17981, (article 2032?) This hybrid aircraft is designated SR-71C and consists of the wing and rear section of YF-12A, 60-6934, and the forward fuselage from a static test specimen. This pilot trainer first flew 14 March 1969 and still serves today when '956 is down for deep maintenance.

Note*
Of the 20 remaining SR-71s, one aircraft is 'bailed' by SAC to AFLC at Palmdale. Intelligence requirements coupled with high operating and maintenance costs result in probably nine aircraft being funded for operations each fiscal year. (Two at Mildenhall, two at Kadena and probably four A models and one two-seat pilot trainer at Beale.) The operational requirement is fulfilled by staggering the fleet through a phased rotation, which includes major overhaul and update, flying and storage to evenly distribute airframe hours.

Appendix 2 **The men**

9th SRW Commanders

	Date Assumed	Date Relieved
Col Douglas T Nelson	Jan 1966	Dec 1966
Col William R Hayes	Jan 1967	Jun 1969
Col Charles E Minter	Jun 1969	Jun 1970
Col Harold E Confer	Jul 1970	May 1972
Col Jerome F O'Malley	May 1972	May 1973
Col Patrick J Halloran	May 1973	Jun 1975
Col John H Storrie	Jul 1975	Sept 1977
Col Michael Kidder	Sept 1977	Jan 1979
Col Dale Shelton	Feb 1979	Jul 1980
Col David Young	Jul 1980	Jul 1982
Col Thomas S Pugh	Jul 1982	Jul 1983
Col Hector Freese	Aug 1983	Jan 1985
Col David H Pinsky	Jan 1985	Present

It is perhaps of passing interest to note that the first seven commanders were all promoted to General—has the mystique faded?

9th SRW Vice Wing Commanders

	Date Assumed	Date Relieved
Col Marvin L Speer	Jan 1966	Dec 1966
Col Charles F Minter	Dec 1966	June 1969
Col Harold E Confer	Jun 1969	Jun 1970
Col James E Anderson	Jul 1970	Dec 1971
Col Dennis B Sullivan	Dec 1971	Jul 1972
Col Patrick J Halloran	Jul 1972	Jun 1973
Col Donald A Walbrecht	Jun 1973	May 1974
Col John H Storrie	Jun 1974	Jun 1975
Col Robert D Beckel	Jun 1975	Sept 1976
Col Lyman M Kidder	Oct 1976	Sep 1977
Col William E Lawson III	Sept 1977	Jan 1979
Col David G Young	Feb 1979	Jul 1980
Col Thomas S Pugh	Jul 1980	Jul 1982
Col Lonnie S Liss	Jul 1982	Jul 1983
Col David H Pinsky	Jan 1983	Jan 1985
Col Robert B McConnell	Jan 1985	Present

Commanders of the 99th SRS

	Date Assumed	Date Relieved
Lt Col John B Boynton	Jun 1966	Dec 1967
Lt Col Robert G Sowers	Jan 1967	Mar 1968
Lt Col John C Kennon	Apr 1968	Nov 1969
Lt Col Harlon A Hain	Nov 1969	Mar 1971

Commanders of the 1st SRS

Lt Col William R Griner	Jan 1966	Mar 1966
Lt Col Harold E Confer	Apr 1966	Oct 1966
Lt Col Raymond Haupt	Nov 1966	Jul 1967
Lt Col Alan L Hichew	Jul 1967	Sep 1968
Lt Col Patrick J Halloran	Sept 1968	Nov 1969
Lt Col James L Watkins	Dec 1969	Mar 1971
Lt Col Harlon A Hain	Apr 1971	Jul 1971
Lt Col Larry S DeVall	Jul 1971	Jan 1972
Lt Col Kenneth S Collins	Jan 1972	Jun 1972
Lt Col George M Bull	Jun 1972	Jul 1973
Lt Col Brian K McCallum	Jul 1973	Jan 1974
Lt Col James H Shelton Jr	Jan 1974	Aug 1975
Lt Col Raphael S Samey	Aug 1975	Jun 1977
Lt Col Adolphus H Bledsoe Jr	Jul 1977	Dec 1978
Lt Col Randoph B Hertzog	Dec 1978	Dec 1979
Lt Col Richard H Graham	Jan 1980	Jul 1981
Lt Col Eldon W Joersz	Aug 1981	Jul 1983
Lt Col Alan B Cirino	Jul 1983	Aug 1985
Lt Col Joseph Kinego	Aug 1985	Present

Listed below are the names of every pilot and RSO to have flown the SR-71 whilst serving with the 1st or 99th SRS.

John Storrie/'Coz' Mallozzi
Gray Sowers/'Butch' Shefield
Al Hichew/Tom Schmittou
'Pete' Collins/Connie Seagroves
John Kennon/Cecil Braden
Bill Campbell/Al Pennington
Pat Halloran/Mort Jarvis
Buddy Brown/Dave Jensen
Dale Shelton/Larry Boggess
Jerry O'Malley/Ed Payne
Don Walbrecht/Phil Loignon
Earle Boone/Dewain Vick
Tony Bavacqua/Jerry Crew
Jim Watkins/Dave Dempster
Ben Bowles/Jimmy Fagg
Larry DeVall/Clyde Shoemaker
Bob Spencer/'Keith' Branham
Brian McCallum/Bob Locke
Roy St Martin/Jim Carnochan
George Bull/Bill McNeer
Bob Powell/Bill Kendrick
Charlie Daubs/Bob Roetciseonder
Bobby Campbell/Jon Kraus
Abe Kardong/Jim Kogler
Nick Maier/Garry Coleman
Willie Lawson/Gil Martinez
Dave Frehauf/Al Payne
Jim Hudson/Norbert Budzinski
Harlon Hain/Richard Sheffield
Tom Estes/Dewain Vick
Jim Shelton/Tom Schmutton
Dave Cobb/Myron Gantt
Tom Pugh/Ron Rice

Denny Bush/Phil Loignon
Randy Hertzog/John Carnochan
Dave Cobb/Reg Blackwell
Bob Cunningham/'GT' Morgan
Ty Judkins/Clyde Shoemaker
Jim Sullivan/Noel Widdifield
Bob Gunther/Tom Allocca
Carl Haller/John Fuller
'Pat' Bledsoe/Reg Blackwell
Mark Gersten/Lee Ransom
Harold Adams/Bill Machorck
Bob Helt/Larry Elliott
'Al' Joersz/John Fuller
Jim Willson/Jim Douglass
Maury Rosenberg/Don Bullock
Joe Kinego/Roger Jacks
Al Cirino/Bruce Liebman
Jay Murphy/John Billingsley
Rich Graham/Don Emmons
Bob Crowder/John Morgan
Tom Alison/'JT' Vida
Buz Carpenter/John Murphy
Jack Veth/Bill Keller
Bill Grominger/Chuck Sober
'BC' Thomas/Jay Reid
Tom Keck/Tim Shaw
Dave Peters/Ed Bethart
Lee Shelton/Barry Mac Kean
Rich Young/Russ Szczepanik
Gil Bertelson/Frank Stampf
Rich Judson/Frank Kelly
Nevin Cunningham/Geno Quist
Jerry Glasser/Mac Hornbaker
Maury Rosenberg/'ED' McKim
Rick McCrary/Dave Lawrence
Bernie Smith/Denny Whalen
Gil Luloff/Bob Coats
Les Dyer/Dan Greenwood
Bill Burk/Tom Henichek

Note: Current personnel cannot be listed for security reasons.

It is believed that the 1st SRS maintains between 10–12 crews with in excess of 100 hours on type. When they have completed the 13 'Initial Qual' portions of the simulator programme two or three crews would be working through the Mission Qualified (MQ) phase of their training, gaining hours and experience in readiness to maintain operational staffing levels as 'old heads' leave on completion of their tour. An alpha numeric system is used by the 1st SRS to identify a crew and its level of experience on type. In the 'old days', senior officers in the wing and squadron would occasionally fly and for that purpose were allocated the initials 'ST' prior to a two digit crew number. But today only the initials NRE and S are used, eg:

N-01 indicates that crew 01 are N—not ready for operations. This designation would probably be applied to a crew on satisfactory completion of MQ-2, from which point the pilot and RSO are teamed up and the former would have accrued about 30 hours on type.

R-01 indicates that our crew have been certified R—ready for operations. Although there are no hard and fast rules for this, it appears to occur after MQ-6 with the pilot having logged about 60 hours on type.

E-01 indicates that the crew are now considered E—senior.

This only occurs after the pilot has logged at least 100 hours on type and flown the aircraft operationally on their first TDY.

S-01 indicates that the crew have become S—select. These 'high-timers' have reached an extremely high state of expertise; there being perhaps only two crews in the squadron with this designation and their duties are invariably standardisation and evaluation—stan/eval, examining crews and ensuring that the highest standards of airmanship are maintained.

Appendix 3

Significant dates during the development and deployment of the Blackbird family.

Between 21 April 1958 and 29 August 1959 Kelly Johnson proposes A-1 through A-12 designs to the CIA and US Air Force

29 August 1959: Lockheed A-12 design declared winner

16/17 March 1960: Kelly Johnson proposes interceptor version of A-12

26 April 1962: maiden flight of A-12 from Groom Lake by Lou Schalk

4 June 1962: Air Force evaluation team review SR-71 mockup

July 1962: J58 completes Pre-Flight Rating Test

27/28 December 1962: Lockheed placed on contract to build six production SR-71s

January 1963: first J58 installed in an A-12

24 May 1963: first A-12 lost in accident

7 August 1963: maiden flight of YF-12 from Groom Lake by Jim Eastham

29 February 1964: President Lyndon B Johnson announces existence of 'Oxcart' programme

25 July 1964: President Johnson announces existence of the SR-71

29 October 1964: SR-71 prototype delivered to Palmdale

14 December 1964: General John Ryan announces that SR-71s are to be based at Beale AFB

18 December 1964: first engine run of the SR-71 prototype

21 December 1964: SR-71 taxi tests take place

22 December 1964: maiden flight of SR-71 from Palmdale by Bob Gilliland

1 May 1965: YF-12 sets new world speed and altitude records

1 June 1965: SR-71/YF-12 Test Force formed at Edwards AFB

7 July 1965: first two T-38 companion trainers arrive at Beale AFB

2 November 1965: maiden flight of the SR-71B from Palmdale by Bob Gilliland and Bill Weaver

6 January 1966: US Air Force takes delivery of first SR-71B

7 January 1966: first SR-71B arrives at Beale AFB

25 January 1966: first SR-71A lost in accident

10 May 1966: US Air Force takes delivery of its first SR-71A

25 June 1966: 4200 SRW at Beale is redesignated, along with its component squadrons

30 July 1966: loss of A-12 60-6941 and subsequent death of Ray Torick signals end of A-12/D-21 programme

13 April 1967: 9th SRW loses its first SR-71A

11 January 1968: only SR-71B loss to-date

April 1968: first operational sortie of SR-71 over Southeast Asia

5 June 1968: final operational flight of A-12 ends tragically with loss of both pilot and aircraft

1 November 1968: 9th SRW receives the AF Outstanding Unit Award

14 March 1969: maiden flight from Palmdale of the only hybrid SR-71C

11 December 1969: first flight of YF-12 during a joint USAF/NASA flight test programme

16 January 1970: SR-71/YF-12 Test Force redesignated 4786 Test Squadron

1 April 1971: 99th SRS is deactivated as an SR-71 unit

26 April 1971: an SR-71A completes a 15,000 mile non-stop flight around the USA in 10 hours 30 mins (64/17968)

12 May 1972: 4786 Test Squadron is deactivated at Edwards

May 1973: loss of '978 is last SR-71 loss at time of writing

12 October 1973: SR-71A takes off from Griffiss AFB, New York, on first of ten reconnaissance flights over Middle East during Yom Kippur War

1 September 1973: SR-71 sets new world speed record between New York and London

13 September 1973: SR-71 sets new world speed record between London and Los Angeles

27/28 July 1976: SR-71s set new world speed and altitude records

March 1979: Det 4 of the 9th SRW is formed at RAF Mildenhall

31 October 1979: NASA flight test programme ends

7 November 1979: final flight of YF-12 when '935 delivered to USAF Museum

1 August 1981: 4029th SRTS formed at Beale AFB to train SR-71 and U-2/TR-1 crews

7 November 1984: first operational sortie of SR-71 over Nicaragua

15 April 1986: two SR-71s from RAF Mildenhall undertake post-strike reconnaissance of Libya after Operation Eldorado Canyon

Index